T0322146

the
path
to
self-love

the

path

to

self-love

heal your heart,

set healthy

boundaries

& unlock your inner

strength

Ruby Dhal

RIDER

Rider, an imprint of Ebury Publishing
20 Vauxhall Bridge Road
London SW1V 2SA

Rider is part of the Penguin Random House group of companies
whose addresses can be found at global.penguinrandomhouse.com

First published by Rider in 2024

www.penguin.co.uk

A CIP catalogue record for this book is available from the British Library

ISBN 9781846047657

Printed and bound in Great Britain by Clays Ltd, Elcograf S.p.A.

The authorised representative in the EEA is Penguin Random House
Ireland, Morrison Chambers, 32 Nassau Street, Dublin D02 YH68

Penguin Random House is committed to a sustainable future for our
business, our readers and our planet. This book is made from
Forest Stewardship Council® certified paper.

To my family, who have walked every step of
this self-love journey with me.

To my husband, who has always
pushed me to reach for the stars.

contents

When the difficult days pass, promise me you won't forget how courageous you were when things got hard — how honest you were with your pain. How your hands held your heart with a gentleness that couldn't be matched. Promise me you won't forget the sunsets that left you glowing gold on evenings that felt too heavy on your shoulders. Promise me that you won't forget the light that you found bubbling inside when you couldn't find it anywhere else. When the difficult days pass, promise me you won't forget how easy it was to give up — but you never did. Promise me you won't forget that you gave yourself a new life. You found new friends. Took adventures. You let your laughter reach inside you and make you warm again. You gave love another chance. You didn't let your past define you. You let it build you. Promise me you won't forget how much the difficult days took out of you, and just how much you poured back in.

exercise

Before you begin your self-love journey, think about something you're struggling with that you would like to overcome by the end of the book. For example:

* ✳   'I struggle with putting my foot down and saying no.'

* ✳   'I can't move on from the person who broke my heart.'

* ✳   'I don't know what I deserve.'

* ✳   'A friend is hurting me, and I don't know how to tell her.'

* ✳   'I'm grieving from the death of a family member.'

* ✳   'I realised I'm experiencing emotional abuse, and I don't know how to deal with it.'

* ✳   'I recently lost my job, and it's caused me to have low self-esteem.'

Now, write it down on a piece of paper, type it on your phone or memorise it. But don't forget it. We will come back to it later.

introduction to self-love

You will have experiences that change the course of your life forever. These experiences can be uncomfortable. They can trigger you, or cause hurt from earlier wounds to rise, plunging you back into the past. It could be something you've failed at. Or a loss. Someone close to you has gone forever, or you're the one who's left. It could be a cluster of bad experiences that keep reoccurring until a situation finally comes crashing down. Or it could be just one event, one small significant event, one moment of impact that changes the *before* and *after* of your life forever.

I had such a moment of impact, and it transformed my life, for better or worse. Many years later, it became the catalyst for my discovery of how self-love can shape our healing journeys, give us the courage to move on and empower us to manifest long-lasting happiness.

SELF-LOVE CAN HEAL YOUR HEART

I was only four when I lost my mum forever.

When I replay it in my mind, a memory as vivid as the one of what I had for dinner yesterday, I'm aware that my entire life was guided by that single event. That one moment in time where the *before* and *after* of my existence were worlds apart, even though the *'before'* had lasted just four years.

Experiencing a devastating trauma at a young age marked the start of my first healing journey.

A journey that set off all the others.

This book comes from there.

It's a result of years of me healing from this trauma and moving forward from a difficult past.

Without this harrowing childhood experience, I would've never learned how empowering self-love is for us to heal. This book is a testament to why I came to that conclusion, and how important it is that I share the wisdom that I've gained over the years with those who need it the most: *you, my reader*. This book is a guide to the many ways in which self-love can be the answer to the questions that you have about healing your heart and flourishing in all areas of your life.

As you make your way through this book, you will see the incredible benefits of self-love in healing your heart, but it doesn't stop there. Self-love encourages you to set healthy boundaries, it allows you to thrive in your relationships and it gives you the courage to conquer your daily challenges. The path to self-love is not easy, but once you start that journey, you'll realise that self-love is the answer to all the questions you've had until now about manifesting your greatest adventure, which is: ***a life that you look forward to living***.

Self-love taught me that even though I couldn't do much about the pain that I was handed, I could do a lot with it.

How to Use This Book

Have you ever had that experience where you explain something tedious to your friend? You go over and over the details of a particular exchange that you can't seem to forget. Then your friend comes out with the simplest, clearest response ever, and you end up saying:

'Wow. I never thought of it that way. That makes *so much sense*.'

That is what this book is. That 'makes so much sense' moment with a friend that puts it all into perspective.

In this book, I will guide you through the topics that will come up time and time again on your self-love journey. You will find **journal prompts** and **reflective exercises** to do as you flip through the pages. These will encourage you to apply self-love to your daily life, and they will help you to achieve long-lasting happiness *through your actions*.

To make the most of this book, get a brand-new journal to jot down important points, and to complete the exercises/journal prompts.

Self-love is deeply engrained in every aspect of your life, and I try to do justice to all the curves of your experiences. In this book, there are conversations about self-love and healing journeys, the different types of traumas that can spark those healing journeys and the importance of relationships in practising self-love. You will learn how to set effective boundaries in your relationships and address everyday challenges and stumbling blocks, until you finally celebrate this path to self-love that you've embarked on by writing your own individual self-love manifesto.

This is a practical book and I encourage you to read and absorb, but also to create your own self-love practices as you make your way through these pages – for now and for the future.

When you pick up a book like this, I assume that you want to meet the author and truly get to know them. That you want to gain not only insight but also a connection with them. A sacred bond. Where you leave feeling like you can take on anything, because someone who you resonate with managed to, so there's no limit to what you can do either. For this reason, this book is personal. I want you and I to connect on a deeper level.

I won't be prescriptive or tell you what to do to magically transform your life. I won't give you a PowerPoint presentation. I won't advise you to look in the mirror and chant '*I love myself*' repeatedly until you start to look cross-eyed. Because those things have never worked for me.

But do you know what has worked for me?

Having honest chats with *my people*. Sitting down and laying out my thoughts, sharing my experiences with those who feel like home, then coming out from those conversations feeling so understood.

I want you to use this book to see your thoughts and emotions differently. Like that peaceful afternoon spent with a close friend who helps you figure out how to come out from a mess, and even if you don't figure it out, *you come out happier*. Relieved that you've let it all out. That is how you use this book. Just like that tranquil time spent alone or that late night phone call with your best friend, which puts it all into perspective. Just like that pat on your back or the shoulder that you can rest your head on, this book is something you can rely on when you're healing and hurting.

When you're coping and fighting.

When you're trying to move forward but feeling as though you're getting nowhere.

When you're coming across too many stumbling blocks and have been stuck in one place for way too long.

That is when you pick up this book. That is when you pick up this book.

Defining Self-Love

Self-Love: A Definition

*Self-love is a significant tool that you can use in your healing journey, where you act to improve the quality of your life and achieve long-lasting happiness. To do this, you must have a healthy relationship with yourself and your loved ones. **Self-love is living with an intention to nourish your life**.*

*To clarify further, self-love isn't feeling **unconditional love** towards yourself. Self-love doesn't mean making yourself a priority or putting your needs first **every single day**. Self-love is striking a delicate balance between the internal and the external, between what matters to you and what makes you happy. Self-love is being honest about who you are, accepting your imperfections and knowing that you can get it wrong sometimes, and that's okay.*

When I say that self-love isn't 'unconditional', I mean that you can't love yourself without having any expectations from yourself. You can't love yourself without any strings, because that wouldn't do justice to the path of self-love.

Your relationship with yourself is like the relationship that you share with others, such as your parents, your close friends or a romantic partner. You love the people close to you, but it would be inaccurate to say that you love them without having any expectations from them, because that's not how relationships work. If the people you loved kept letting you down or acting in a way that harmed you, and they didn't respect or even listen to you when you voiced your needs, over time your love for them would lessen, or even disappear. Perhaps in the case of parents, you would still be there for them out of a sense of duty, attachment or habit, but you probably wouldn't love them in the same way – or at all.

Similarly, to say that you can love yourself without having any expectations from yourself would be inaccurate, because this would mean that you can keep letting yourself down, or acting in a harmful way towards yourself but still love yourself the same. When you love yourself, you owe it to yourself to make certain positive changes that contribute to your mental, emotional and physical well-being. Unconditional love means loving yourself without needing or wanting anything in return, but the path to self-love encourages you to have a balanced relationship with yourself where you love yourself but are committed to taking care of your needs as well.

SELF-LOVE IS MORE THAN A HASHTAG

'Self-love' has become an enormous part of our daily lingo and is scattered through our everyday conversations. We advise our friends to use 'self-love' when they're struggling, even if we don't fully understand their circumstances. For instance, when your best friend tells you about an argument that she had with her controlling partner, and you advise her to *'Love yourself, girl, and cut him off.'* The word 'self-love' also frequently appears in our social media captions and hashtags: *'Just having a self-care day, #bubblebath #putyourselffirst #selflovematters'*, or, *'A book and me is all I need, #caramellatte #takecareofyourself #selflovefirst'*.

I'd need more than two hands to count the number of times I've opened TikTok to find another 'self-care day vlog' posted by an influencer, sprinkled with shots of painfully early wake-ups, even more painful-looking yoga positions, coffeemaking ASMR (this is both weird and alluring), a bunch of *wholesome* and *healthy* meals in cafés, walks to the park and runs in the middle of nowhere, as though it were completely normal to place a tripod in a random street and record yourself running back and forth. Well, it's the new normal.

I'm not complaining, because those vlogs can be so therapeutic both for the people who post them, and the people who watch them, and I'm all about other people practising self-care and living their best lives. I'm merely pointing out that there is another – incredibly important – side to self-love that we often seem to overlook. A side that can change your life for the better. It's that side of self-love that we will focus on here. Through practising self-love, you *can live your best life* – but self-love doesn't have to be limited to running in the park and early morning yoga.

I'm not saying these activities aren't important, but there is so much more to self-love than we may see around us, and this book will help you access those forms of self-love, because you will need them on your own healing journey.

Self-love is a balancing act between doing the fun things and practising the hard ones. Self-love is running yourself a long, hot bath. Self-love is ordering a takeaway and putting on a movie on Netflix. Self-love is meeting up with old friends, or new ones, and having engaging conversations. Self-love is also setting boundaries and saying 'no'. Self-love is letting yourself cry. Self-love is going for a run to the park on good days and spending the morning under the covers on bad ones. Self-love is having difficult conversations. Self-love is letting go. Self-love is going to the theatre with your friends, followed by a fancy dinner. Self-love is also taking time away from everyone. Self-love is buying yourself some new clothes. Self-love is leaving your current job and taking a break. Self-love is going travelling, but self-love is also coming home. On days when you feel the happiest, self-love is going to the beach and having a picnic. Self-love is dancing in the rain. But on days when you feel low, self-love is getting under the covers early and going to sleep. Self-love is listening to health podcasts and self-love is being by yourself. When it comes to self-love, no one can tell you exactly what to do. It's all about your perspective and where each new day takes you — because sometimes you feel like hiding away from everyone, and sometimes you feel ready to take over the world.

EASY OR TOUGH SELF-LOVE?

Watching a movie, spending time with friends or going for a walk outside are all part of self-love – they're the things that come to mind straight away when we think of self-love, and they're an important part of finding joy every day. They promote happiness and create a healthy balance in many people's lives, but they can be categorised as 'easy self-love'. This form of self-love needs to be separated from the self-love that we're talking about in this book; the kind of self-love that can change your life forever: 'tough self-love'.

Think of these as two sides of the same coin. You can't perform one without the other, and each side is important in its own way. But remember, it's the tough stuff that allows you to get to the easy stuff. It's the tough stuff that is the most life-changing.

Easy self-love means improving your mental, emotional and physical well-being through activities that lift your mood, increase your joy or otherwise improve your vibe. Whatever you want to call it. For instance, to improve your mental health, you meditate, journal, travel, cook, read, take a walk, etc. To improve your emotional health, you meet up with your loved ones and have adventures, and to improve your physical health, you go to the gym, eat healthy, go to sleep on time, do yoga.

Filing these things under 'easy self-love' doesn't mean that they don't take much out of you. They can. Easy self-love means doing anything that *makes you feel good* and that is done with the intention to improve the quality of your life. Often the 'feel good' sensation can come much later, but the intention is always there; for example, when you lift weights at the gym, it's painful at first but worth it for the high you get afterwards. When you practise easy self-love, you become aware that you're doing something to take care of yourself.

In comparison to tough self-love, easy self-love is *simpler*. We all see it, hear about it, scroll through our Instagram feeds and watch others indulging in it. We believe that we know what self-love is when we come across it.

But tough self-love isn't as apparent.

Practising tough self-love means **doing the hard work**. For instance, asking yourself the difficult, exhausting questions, sitting alone with your icy thoughts, trying to unpick the emotions that lie underneath, going to therapy, perhaps joining an AA meeting and admitting that you have a drinking problem, cutting off people, setting your expectations, apologising, getting closure, rewinding the reel of your past to pluck out traumatic events that have caused you to have low self-esteem or trust issues, or to become non-committal, and trying to iron them out so you can move *past the past*. Make sense?

Tough self-love is *tough*.

Both easy and tough self-love practices are based on the intention to take care of yourself – although with tough practices, it's a lot more indirect. With easy self-love, you acknowledge that you've had a rough day, so you go to see your friend for dinner and unwind. With tough self-love, if you've had a rough day and you have an appointment with your therapist later, that will take a lot out of you, and you probably won't feel good in the moment. Practising easy self-love usually elicits positive emotions (such as happiness, laughter, excitement, love) and practising tough self-love usually elicits negative emotions (such as sadness, a feeling of loss, tears, regret, guilt), which can be harder to do.

But the end result of tough self-love will bring you long-lasting happiness, allowing you to make peace with your past and encouraging you to exercise easy self-love to improve the quality of your life.

Our culture has put a lot of emphasis on self-love by highlighting only the easy activities. We've started to believe that the easy stuff is all we need to do to soul-search, or heal from our trauma, or become at one with ourselves. But that's not true. By comparison, there's not much emphasis or value given to the tough form of self-love, which usually takes a lot out of you but can be more life-changing in the long run. Don't get me wrong, I love an iced caramel latte and a book in my favourite café just as much as the next person – and it really is my favourite form of self-care. But the only reason I can enjoy this is because I've done the hard work and continue to do so. I've exercised tough self-love and continue to make the most of it, and that is why I can enjoy the 'easy' stuff now and reap its benefits.

journal

What easy self-love practices do you take part in? E.g., go for daily walks, catch up with loved ones, do early-morning yoga, go to a café and grab an iced latte.

What tough self-love practices do you take part in? E.g., go for therapy sessions, set boundaries, have honest yet difficult conversations, get closure, reflect on your trauma.

Do you currently practise more easy or more tough self-love exercises?

Why do you think this is?

How do these make you feel?

You might also be wondering why our definition of self-love includes relationships. Why do you need other people when practising self-love? We'll explore this more in Chapter Three (page 67), but for now, it's important to remember that in our pursuit of practising easy self-love in today's world, we've pushed aside the value of our relationships. This is because in our practice of self-love, and how we see others practising it, we tend to prioritise ourselves by focusing on solitary pursuits. We don't think about the many activities and practices that bring us joy which include other people. Spending time with others is a form of self-love, but in today's world, we seem to have forgotten this.

Improving the quality of your life and manifesting long-lasting happiness through self-love isn't achievable without meaningful relationships. Think about it. When you've had a rough day and you call your best friend, you instantly feel better, either because they've given you advice or because they've made you laugh and forget about your problems. The same applies when you go to see your friends or spend time with your family. Seeing your people, the ones who are good for you, can do so much to lift your energy and improve your day (more on energies later in Chapter Five, page 123).

> As you set off on the path to self-love on your
> healing journey, don't let your vision be blurred
> by social media constructs/cultural constructs
> of self-love that do more to isolate you than
> to bring you closer to yourself through the
> power of your relationships.

The Power of Self-Love

There are a few questions I'm expecting you to have in your mind about the power of self-love, among others.

How can self-love help me heal my heart and live my best life?

What can self-love do for my healing?

Why is self-love important for me to thrive in life?

Since this book is about the power of self-love in healing your heart and enabling you to live your best life, these questions will be answered as the book progresses, but for now, I've summarised a few ways in which self-love can improve your life. Don't worry if these points seem a little ambiguous, as they will be elaborated on throughout the book.

Firstly, self-love gives you power over your life. Through practising self-love, you regain the power that you've given away to things or people in the past. For instance, I can control how healthy my mind and body are by going to the gym and reading every day. This confidence seeps into other areas of my life where I start asserting my power too, such as in the boundaries that I set and the people that I let into my safe circle. It's okay if you don't know how to apply boundaries yet, because this book will guide you through.

Self-love encourages you to put yourself first when it matters. Note that I didn't say 'always' – I didn't even say 'most of the time'. Put yourself first only when it matters, because that's when it makes the most difference. I put myself first when it comes to my dreams, goals and daily habits, but there have been occasions where I've put my loved ones first. On those occasions, putting myself first doesn't do anything for me – but putting them first does a lot for *their* well-being. Putting others first and contributing to their happiness makes me happy. When my loved ones are okay, I feel ten times better. After all, energy is infectious.

Self-love allows you to enjoy better relationships with others. We will swim into this ocean in Chapter Five. But for now, I'd say that self-love and relationships are so deeply entwined that if you feel stuck in your life, the first area to improve should be your relationships with others. Whether that means catching your mum for brunch or giving your friend a call on the way home, or making up with someone you fell out with, taking the first step will make all the difference. Try it!

And, finally, self-love encourages you to treat yourself with kindness and compassion, and this makes the process of healing gentler. When you treat yourself with compassion, you allow yourself to go through the highs and lows of healing, you're patient with your heart as you hold the pain and learn to move forward with it, and you stop comparing your progress to others', because your journey is *yours only*.

There are myriad other ways in which practising self-love can transform your life, and this book goes into many of them in depth for you. I hope you make use of this incredible tool and succeed in achieving your dreams and goals, enjoying nourishing relationships and conquering your daily challenges.

Self-love helps you flourish by encouraging you to put yourself first when needed, set healthy boundaries, create a balance in your relationships and treat yourself with warmth and care.

1. Write the word 'self-love' in the centre of a page and draw a bubble around it.

2. From the bubble, draw out arrows, and at the end of those arrows, write down what reminds you of self-love. Examples include, 'putting myself first', 'setting boundaries', 'having honest conversations', 'saying "no"', 'having a self-care day', 'watching Netflix', 'reading', etc.

3. After you've written at least ten words/phrases, flick to a new page and write a description of self-love for each of them. For instance, 'Self-love is grabbing a coffee and going on a walk.'

4. Number these in terms of priority, with 1 being the least important expression of self-love and 10 being the most important.

5. At the start of a new week, carry out at least two actions that are between numbers 7 and 10, and at least four actions that are between 3 and 6. You're welcome to change the priority of these actions as the weeks go on.

6. At the end of the week, write down how you feel.

7. Next week, start it all over again.

chapter 1

understanding the healing journey

Remember those moments of impact I spoke about at the start of the introduction? The ones where your life before and after that event is never the same, where the *you* at the start of the experience and the *you* after can be worlds apart. These moments of impact often mark the beginning of a healing journey.

Maybe you're trying to move on but can't. Maybe you find yourself stuck in one place. Maybe you've *just figured out* that this journey you're on is one of healing, and you want to know more. Maybe this is what led you to picking up this book; maybe you're looking for answers that you haven't been able to find. A part of you knows that you have the strength to move on – but you still can't figure out how. This is where self-love comes in.

we can't control some of the experiences we undergo, but we can control how we react to them, and who we become in the face of adversity.

A healing journey begins when you experience a traumatic or wounding event. It's something your mind, soul and body must go through after a painful experience. Often, you're aware that you're on that journey because you actively want to mend the part of you that has been harmed, but you could also be healing from something for years before you realise the journey you're on. For instance, perhaps you're healing from a failure that you had aged ten, which has led you to always strive for success and causes you to have really low self-esteem when you don't meet your own expectations. Until you grasp where this harmful drive for success comes from, you won't be able to heal from that initial failure.

Each event of this sort in your life sets off a new healing journey. Often these experiences can overlap – hence, the journeys can also overlap. For instance, perhaps you're moving on from your first heartbreak, as well as the one you most recently had, or you're recovering from your parents' divorce, and now the loss of your job, or you're coping with the death of a grandparent, and your childhood best friend moving thousands of miles away.

When you're healing, you can reach a more tender place in some journeys and still be in rougher places in others.

For example, you can be in a better, calmer place in relation to the loss of your job and be actively interviewing for a new one, but perhaps you're still not in a good place regarding your parents' broken marriage. You might have gotten over your best friend moving away but maybe you still can't get over losing your grandparent.

My first healing journey began when I lost my mum, and this was my most difficult healing journey because it wasn't just my life that fell apart after she died – my dad's life, my brother's life, my extended family, her family, we were all in pieces after that. Since then, I've had many healing journeys, and I'll speak about them in this book, the most significant one being the one that I had at 21 which sparked my desire to move on from a past that had been clawing at my heart for nearly two decades.

> Healing is a gradual, uneven road which you can stumble and even fall on. Healing isn't simple, easy or linear, so you could take one step forward and three steps back, but this doesn't mean that you haven't made progress overall.

Maybe we are healing our entire lives. From our firsts, and from our lasts. From our losses. From the broken friendships and broken hearts. From the childhood experiences that we wish we could forget. Maybe we never truly reach an 'end point' in our healing because we were not meant to. Because healing isn't an upward curve but a line that staggers through the tunnels of love, loss and growth – which we must try our best to sail through, not out of. Maybe our healing isn't about reaching somewhere but about moving – forward, onwards, away from the trauma and the cutting wounds of the past. Maybe it was never about forgetting our difficult days and lonesome nights but about understanding how to take them forward with us. It wasn't about living through the pain but allowing it to move with us – by becoming a lesson for growth. Maybe we spend our entire lives running away from the things that we were meant to hold on to, the things that – instead of being a weight on our back – were meant to be the tools that we would keep in our rucksack and take out at every bend of the adventure we call life.

COMMON MISCONCEPTIONS OF HEALING

'You can project healing journeys on a line graph, where the line represents the progress and is headed upwards.'
This isn't true. Healing journeys rise and fall like the sun, and you will see the highs and the lows as you walk them. You won't necessarily be headed up and out of that pain – sometimes you will have a good day and right after that you can have a bad one.

'Healing is prescriptive, so if you carry out X, Y or Z action, then you will heal faster and better.'
Again, this is false. The purpose of healing isn't to transform you or treat you like medicine would, the purpose of healing is to provide you with essential tools, allow you to grow and give you the strength to face all future battles in your life. *Because there will be more.*

'Healing internally is like healing externally, where there's a process and you reach an end point.'
This is false. There is no 'end' to healing because you will always be healing from one experience in your life or another.

Healing is so much more than what you and I
thought it was. Healing is honest, it is raw.
Healing is a journey. Healing is self-acceptance
and moving on, it's understanding yourself in
new ways and, even if you can't, it's trying your
best anyway. And in these healing journeys, you
need to learn to love yourself, in whatever way
you can muster, to truly move on.

People also often have this misconception that healing from an internal wound is like healing from an external one.

Let's consider an external wound first. When you physically injure yourself, you notice a bruise or cut on your body. That cut over time turns into a scab, and the scab peels and leaves a scar. As more time passes, that scar – just like the bruise – fades and disappears, and we use this as a sign that the wound on your body has healed. This process is a result of hundreds of thousands of years of biological evolution. It's our body's way of communicating that our external injuries have repaired themselves, and we can stop being extra careful with that body part and use it as normal.

Our mistake is that we often compare our internal healing journeys to external wounds. We assume that during our healing journey, our internal cut will 'scab', 'peel off', 'leave a scar' and, eventually, that scar will fade over time until it disappears – symbolising the various stages of healing. But that's not how healing works at all. Your internal scars don't fade or disappear with time, *they go forward with you*. Perhaps as time passes, those scars no longer cause you as much pain as they did before – but this is a consequence of you becoming more capable of dealing with the unease rather than the unease itself disappearing.

Time is a powerful device, allowing you to let go of the past. As more time passes between the event that started your healing journey, all the growth, lessons and experiences fill up that time, creating more space between you and the initial event. As a result, you forget how much pain that experience caused you and you move forward. But, once again, forgetting the pain doesn't mean that the pain itself has disappeared.

When we're healing, pain won't affect us as it did before, but the scars in our hearts go with us.

exercise

Are you currently on one or more healing journeys?

Write them down in your journal in the following format:

✳ Event that started this journey

✳ Roughly when this journey started (if you can remember)

✳ How you feel in this journey right now

Jot down at least two journeys, but there's no limit to how many healing journeys one is on, and this is your safe space to share as many healing journeys as you want. You're the only one who will read your journal.

By the end of this exercise, you will have an idea of where you are, emotionally, on those initial experiences.

Pick out the journey that still causes you pain. Pick out the journey in which you're struggling. You may have more than one.

For the rest of the book, for any healing-related exercise, refer to this journey.

I need you to know that healing and hurting often go hand in hand, and that the journey is messy, fluctuating and flooded with enough challenges that make you want to give up. But life is beautiful, experiences lace your path with colour and people — they make living worthwhile. I need you to know that you don't need to have everything figured out. You need to focus on your own timescale rather than on what other people are doing with their lives. You need to measure your growth and progress in relation to your previous experiences and struggles instead of others' success. Everyone's journey is different, and it's only when you appreciate this difference that you can accept everything that your life brings you. You need to focus on you. I need you to know that you must direct all your energy towards your mind and soul with the hope that it will allow some magic to form. I need you to know that you will continue to learn today, tomorrow and in the days that follow. You will have experiences that have the power to break you, and bring you joy, and enlighten you in new ways. I need you to know that you will keep learning until you feel wiser, stronger and whole. And even then, you will continue learning — because there is so much in every curve of this world that you can discover, and there is so much that you need to know before you can say that you know enough. And even when you say that 'I know enough', you will keep learning. You will keep going. You will keep growing along the way.

MEMORIES ARE IMPORTANT FOR GROWTH

If your internal scars disappeared with time, then you would forget about them. You would forget about who you were when you had those experiences. You would forget the lessons you learned, the transformation you had and the person that you became during those healing journeys, losing an essential part of who you are.

In addition to the smaller ones, I've been on two major healing journeys (first at the age of 4, the second at 21) that have taught me so much over the years. When you ask me about my healing journey at 21, I'll say, *'I'm okay. I'm great, in fact.'* But this doesn't mean that I've forgotten all about what I went through. If the scars that I had at 21 were to fade away completely, a lot of what I've gained, and who I am, would fade with them. The only way that I can speak about things as *the me that I am today* is because I can still remember how it felt to be *the me that I was back then*.

The false belief that your internal scars disappear over time also feeds into the idea that *healing is an upward curve*. Healing is linear. *Healing is one-way*. But that's not true. Healing is a few steps forward and a few steps back. Healing is up and down. Healing is feeling both high and low at different times. Especially at the start of your journey – because you have more hard days than easy ones. You have more bad days than good ones. Healing is complicated because *we as humans are complicated*. You can't compare the way you heal externally to the way you heal internally, because for your body to move on it needs to repair itself, and for your heart to move on it needs to string itself together with the threads of your experiences, the very threads that are a result of your trauma and difficult times. Sometimes stringing those threads causes you pain, reminding you that you have a long way to go before you can be okay again.

When you're healing, time is a great tool in helping you forget about the pain that you experienced, but no matter how much time passes, the scars in our hearts will always go with us.

My healing journey from my mum's death is one of the first threads that I used to sew my heart back together, and while I no longer feel sorry for myself when I remember it, I still feel longing for my mum. It's like I've been robbed of a life I could have had. I still feel a pang of regret at the way things turned out for my dad, which is something I will go into detail about later. This doesn't mean that I haven't progressed in healing from that experience, it just means that I will always take a part of that loss with me, no matter where I go. It means that sometimes I will be the happiest person in the world, grateful for everything that I've been blessed with, and sometimes I will feel like the biggest loser because I never got to know the person who birthed me, and the hurt that resulted from that experience is lifelong.

When you're healing, there will be both good and bad days.

On the good days, happiness will fill you up to the top, making it easier to practise self-love and do stuff for yourself, but on the bad days, you will feel empty and numb, and even getting out of bed can seem like the hardest thing to do. On those days you won't be able to take care of yourself. On those days you won't remember what it feels like to love yourself at all.

Healing journeys are flexible and ever changing. Once you accept this, you can start to appreciate the uniqueness of everyone's individual experiences and the importance of self-love as an instrument in your healing journey, one that guides you out of pain and heartache.

journal

If there is one word of advice you would give to the you who was/is at the start of your healing journey, what would it be?

Healing is uncomfortable. It is a long journey. It is going upwards and downwards and taking five steps forward and three steps back. It involves tears and pain and lots of struggle – but it gives you so much back. Lessons. Growth. Wisdom. Closure. Healing isn't like the process of an external scar being replaced with new skin. It's more like a broken ceramic glass being glued together with love, lessons and people. You will heal through broken hearts and healthy relationships. You will heal through jobs, careers and friendships. You will heal as you journey through life. You will heal as you leave the country, start a new adventure and give up on old love. You will keep healing and healing. And it won't stop even when you're older. You will just get wiser. You will just get stronger. Healing won't act as an anaesthetic that makes you numb. Instead, it will bring the pain to you and teach you how to live with it. That is what healing will do. That is what healing will do.

Why Is Self-Love Essential to Unlocking Your Healing Journey?

Until now you probably thought – and rightly so – that loving yourself in the positive, unreserved manner that modern-day culture proposes is not possible when you're healing, especially when you have one of the hard days.

The kind of days that are filled with stinging memories of a past that you wish you could forget, days when you're consumed with self-neglect because you're grieving, days when getting out of bed is too much, days when you don't like your curves and working out seems like a chore, or when even after you work out, you can't help but look in the mirror and notice a little loose skin here and some flab there. Those days make it hard to feel good about yourself. Those days take a lot out of you.

On those days you can't love yourself, or even like yourself. At least not in the way that you think you're expected to.

But now that we've drawn a distinction between easy and tough self-love (page 9), practising self-love not only becomes essential to your healing journey, it revolutionises it.

Because now you can see that in this healing journey of yours, one that is fluctuating and filled with both highs and lows, self-love isn't about the *'unconditional'/'I love me'* mindset. Instead, it is tough. It is messy. It is hard and easy and everything in between. Practising self-love in this way, with all the ups and downs of life, *is both possible and vital*.

Now you can appreciate that when you're healing and practising self-love, you won't always feel good about yourself. Sometimes you will feel bad.

When you're healing, self-love will mean accepting the complexities of your identity and not making excuses for your mistakes.

Self-love will mean letting yourself grow with time and letting the past go. Self-love will mean learning that there are several layers to you, and some that you will struggle to love, such as your inability to lie, the size of your ears or those dips in your lower back. Such as the way your eyes twitch when you're nervous, your stubbornness, your habit of burning yourself out, or your refusal to admit when you're wrong – and that is okay.

When you're healing, self-love will mean growing, changing and embracing your reality. Self-love will mean sometimes being happy and sometimes being sad. Self-love will mean spending a day taking care of yourself and spending a day where you're completely inattentive to your needs, both in the space of a week – because on both days you are existing, you are living. *On both days, you are living.*

> Because when you're healing, self-love allows
> you to be gentler with yourself, especially when
> you have a dip in your journey.

In this healing journey of yours, journalling is an act of self-love. Asserting boundaries is an act of self-love. Spending time with your parents is an act of self-love. Going out and meeting new people is an act of self-love. Giving yourself closure is an act of self-love. Admitting what went wrong in your past relationships is an act of self-love. Spending the day binge-watching your favourite series is an act of self-love. Getting therapy is an act of self-love. Having difficult conversations is an act of self-love. Realising your mistakes, acknowledging them and apologising for the harm you caused *is an act of self-love.*

Self-love transforms your healing journey forever, supporting you in your recovery from all the negative encounters in your past.

Through self-love and acceptance, through being patient and compassionate with yourself, and through changing the narrative in your mind in relation to your experiences, you can guide yourself out of the darkness and reach a comfortable place in your healing journey. You can manifest both light and happiness in your life. You can direct yourself towards all that is good for your heart and beneficial for your soul. You can change your life forever when you give yourself the chance to love yourself.

Self-love isn't prescriptive, either. Just like for healing, there is no one-size-fits-all approach for self-love. Practising tough self-love can bring about so many different lessons and truths for people, and we all live with our truths differently.

To make the most of self-love on your healing journey, embrace the good days and the bad, stop telling yourself to be okay with all your imperfections and appreciate that there can be room for improvement, there can be room to change yourself and become someone new, and that's okay.

I've mentioned before that practising self-love can result in both *positive* and *negative* emotions – through easy and tough activities – and both are okay. They are essential to healing. This is what makes practising both easy and tough activities essential on the path to self-love.

Both tough and easy self-love are significant in your healing, but it's the tough stuff that we've stopped paying attention to – and it is this path to self-love that you'll take in this book. Because maybe you're stuck in your healing. Maybe you're unable to move on.

Maybe you've tried everything under the sun, engaged in all the self-care practices, made new friends, gone travelling, read the books, had the talks and taken the walks, but you still can't come through from your pain. And that's because you've forgotten the hardest truth about healing – that it's complicated, messy and difficult to navigate.

So, how could self-love be uncomplicated?

How could self-love be simple?

How could self-love be *just* the easy stuff and nothing more?

That's just it: self-love *is more*.

For some reason we've created this false idea of healing in our mind, one that takes the following line of thought: 'To heal you should work really, really hard.' And while I don't deny the truth of this sometimes, because certain healing journeys can require so much more energy from us than we ever expected, it isn't true in all cases of healing. Sometimes healing looks like reading a fantasy book. Sometimes healing is writing what you feel down on paper. Sometimes healing means telling someone what you truly think so you can get that weight off your chest. Sometimes healing means separating yourself from the external world with a soft quilt on while you watch your favourite series. Sometimes healing is crying it out, for as long as you need. And sometimes healing is just feeling everything. Entirely. All at once. There is no one type of healing journey, nor can you say that one way of taking care of yourself is more beneficial for your healing than the other. At the end of it, healing can often mean just living, growing and moving on from what was breaking you in whatever way you can. Sometimes healing is waking up one more morning, grateful that you still haven't given up. And sometimes healing is just surviving. It is just surviving. That is what healing is. That is what healing is.

If there were one thing you could change about your life, what would it be?

Is there something that you have the power to do to make this change?

If not, what's stopping you?

How can you counter this?

Are there any alternatives to this situation that would be better?

Despite this, what are you grateful for?

SELF-LOVE HELPS SHIFT YOUR NEGATIVE MINDSET

When you're healing, the biggest thing that self-love can do for you is change your negative mindset. We will build on this in the following chapters and see how it works in action, but for now, know this: if, until now, you had depleting views about where you are in your journey, or you felt that there was no way out – self-love will change that for you. And it doesn't do this straightaway. The shift is gradual, and it happens over weeks and months until the dull graveyard in your mind is replaced with a bright green garden of uplifting thoughts.

The thing about beliefs is that they guide your behaviour and control your actions. At the end of the day, we are our thoughts.

What you believe has a tremendous impact on your reality. For instance, if you believe that you can bungee jump off a cliff and not die then you're more likely to do it, but if you believe that the harness will come off and you will plunge to your death then the likelihood of you ever going bungee jumping is very low. Despite my fear of heights, I've gone bungee jumping, because I wanted to conquer this false belief that I developed for so many years. It was the worst experience of my life, no doubt, but at least I defeated my self-doubt!

Think about the number of times that you've let self-doubt direct your behaviour. The number of times that your low self-confidence about getting on stage, telling someone how you feel or applying for that job has stopped you from carrying out those actions and caused you to miss opportunities that could make your life so much more colourful.

Now, think about how self-love could turn it all around. How those negative thoughts could be transformed into something positive, how 'I can't do it' can become 'I can do this', and 'I'm not loveable' can become 'I deserve love and happiness'. Now, think about how much this could in turn transform your behaviour, both towards yourself and towards the people that you love, and how this could change your life for the better.

> The way that you think about yourself has a huge impact on how you choose to live your life. Instead of telling yourself 'I am unworthy', 'I can't do this', 'I will never move on from this', remind yourself of how far you've come. Tell yourself, 'I can do this', 'Even if I fail, I can give it another shot', 'This is just a phase in my life,

<u>it's not the end of my journey'</u>. Turn your
'I can't' into 'I can' and see how your life
transforms forever.

When you're healing, self-love isn't just about being kinder to yourself but also about turning that kindness into positive actions and behaviour patterns that contribute to the sustenance of your life. When you practise self-love in your healing journey, you push away the dark clouds to welcome a bright blue sky, and you refuse to let your pain define your failures – instead, you view your failures in a way that transforms them into your strengths. And all of this happens through acting on those positive thoughts and beliefs.

exercise

Make a list of your various thoughts that stem from self-doubt.

Have you overcome any of them? If so, which ones?

For the next few weeks, pick one self-doubt a week to overcome.

Come back to your journal and write down how you felt.

Remember, it's not about defeating all your fears, it's about ***wanting*** *to overcome them. It's about* ***trying*** *your best.*

When I was 21, I was overwhelmed by a negative narrative that took over my mind. I dropped out of my teacher training course, was on bad terms with my immediate family and had a breakup with my best friend of seven years, all in the space of a few months. This caused me to have very low self-esteem, and after that whenever something went wrong, I took it as a token of all my failures. But when I adopted self-love in my healing journey, I converted these razor-sharp beliefs into softer ones and saw a tremendous change in my reality. Negative thoughts such as *'It didn't work out because I wasn't worthy'* were converted into *'It didn't work out because there's something better out there for me'*.

> *Thoughts alone don't have the power to miraculously change your reality – your actions play a huge role – but thoughts are the beginning.*

And this didn't happen straightaway. I simmered in hot, stinging emotions for a while because my healing required it. But when that stage in my journey was done and I began reflecting, I noticed the damage that those views were doing to my reality, the relationships it was affecting and the people it was hurting, including myself. It was as though my reality reflected the perception that I had of myself and others. Whenever I was appreciative, good things happened, and whenever I felt bitter, or victimised, things took a turn for the worse.

In the same way, I want you to go forward in this book with positive thoughts in your mind. Kind thoughts. Thoughts that only stem from empathy for yourself. Thoughts that take your growth and well-being into consideration. They are the first step towards the progressive changes that you could make in your healing journey. As Earl Nightingale said, *'Everything begins with an idea.'* An idea is all you need to change your reality.

exercise

The way that you talk to yourself is extremely important in creating your reality and setting the theme of your day-to-day experiences.

For the next week, only speak to yourself in positives, even when something goes wrong. For instance, if you're running late for work, instead of saying, 'That's it, my day is already ruined,' say, 'It's okay. The morning hasn't started right but it will get better, we still have the whole day to go!'

Remember, energy is infectious. You never know what kind of amazing things you can attract with your new positive mindset.

I hope that you want more for yourself. I hope that you see a future where you're living your best life because deep down, you know that it's what you deserve. Despite your insecurities. Despite your fears. Despite all the challenges that you've failed to live up to or the dreams that you're yet to fulfil. I hope that you have faith in what you can achieve in your journey. And I hope that you don't give up. Not now. Not tomorrow. Not ever. Not because giving up is a sign of failure, no — but because giving up is a sign that you no longer believe in that heart of yours. Giving up is a sign that you don't see a point in getting up once more, and that's not what I see for you. I see a bright future for you, and all your wishes coming true. I see love, friendship and a room filled with people celebrating you. I see bright, dewy mornings with a sunrise that brightens up your day, and mild evenings where being alone doesn't make you feel lonely. And I hope that you see all these things for yourself too — because life is both long and short, and it can be very easy to get lost in the months and years that pass you by without realising just how much this life can do for you, and how much you can do for yourself. I hope that you see all of this. I hope that you don't give up on yourself. I hope that you don't give up on yourself.

chapter 2

healing from heartbreak

I need more than two hands to count the number of times I've witnessed a group of friends gather around their heartbroken companion as she bursts into tears, explaining what went wrong in her relationship. The heartbroken friend expects (as most of us do) some useful advice, or affirming words in response to her emotional outburst, but instead she might be told, *'You need to love yourself more.'* The heartbroken friend is stunned into silence, a flush of annoyance in her neck, her eyes puffy and dazed, a slight frown padding her forehead.

Either she didn't expect this response, or she's trying to figure out what her friends are talking about. Because what does that mean? How could the relief to the pain that you're feeling after heartbreak be found in *loving yourself more?*

Loving yourself is a great road to happiness, but isn't the whole idea of grieving a broken heart founded upon this false belief that you're **not** *worthy of loving*, because they rejected you/left you/ didn't want to be with you? Even in cases where you're the one who leaves, perhaps because your partner wasn't making you feel loved, cared for or accepted – you still feel unworthy of love, because it *didn't* work out. There must be something wrong with you(!), and that's why the relationship didn't last.

How can this self-doubt suddenly be solved by loving yourself?

And what does loving yourself look like when you're heartbroken?

> The intensity of the emotions that come with heartbreak can cause severe chest pain like you'd feel during a heart attack and, in rare cases, can even be fatal.

Why Do We Get Heartbroken?

Heartbreak is a form of trauma, and trauma can crack through the foundations of your life. It can change your mindset, affect your emotional stability, reduce your self-esteem and change the strength of all your future relationships. Typically, there are three categories of trauma: acute, chronic and complex. Heartbreak is a type of acute trauma; one significant event that has a deep emotional and psychological impact on you. There are other forms of trauma too, which we will go into in Chapter Three and Chapter Four.

Your heart gets broken when it doesn't work out with someone that you love and care about. Either your long-term relationship has ended, or you were dating someone, and even though you developed feelings, they didn't think that you were *'the one'*, or you've been in love with your childhood best friend for 15 years and they've just announced that they are getting married.

Whatever the reason behind the heartbreak, the pain that you feel once this relationship falls apart is *devastating*. And this stabbing pain that you feel in your chest, the one that chokes you on your words when you're offloading to your mum, cousin or best friend, has been discovered by scientists to be *real*. It's actual pain that can be located in a part of your brain, and it can have a real, hostile effect on your health. For instance, research has found that a person's brain activity when they see a photo of a former lover is similar to their brain activity when they burn their arm. That's incredible.

If you've gone through a heartbreak, or are currently experiencing one, you might have asked yourself: why does it hurt so much? Why can't I move on? Why do I feel a kick in my chest when I think of them? Perhaps at some point you even found it difficult to be taken seriously by your family and friends who had seen you neglect yourself for a long time. Maybe they let you cry to them on the first week, first month or first year while you were/are moving on. And they were great. They were attentive, patient, the best listeners. But eventually they'd also had enough. Perhaps they decided to bluntly tell you to *'Move on – it was just a heartbreak.'* They could no longer empathise with you because they assumed that you would be over it by now. That you *should* be over it by now.

If you haven't experienced this, well done, you've got a great support group, but a lot of us know how it feels if you have, and the next few paragraphs are important for **both** of you, so, keep reading!

Have you been through/are you experiencing a heartbreak?

Where are you in relation to this? E.g., I'm grieving them, I've made my peace, I'm still social media stalking them, I've had my closure, we are still good friends, etc.

We will return to this at the end of this section on heartbreak.

DON'T COMPARE YOUR JOURNEY TO OTHERS'

Heartbreak can often result in an increased feeling of worthlessness. It can make you feel empty and lost. It can cause you to question your decisions and it can make you insecure. Lonely. Scared that you will be single forever (not that this is a bad thing).

When you're struggling to move on, and you notice that you're not healing *'fast enough'* – compared to others – you feel even more bitter about your situation. And if you're being told that it's *'just a heartbreak'*, then you might question whether something is wrong with you which is why you haven't been able to move on from this sooner. This is boosted by the assumption that your friends/social media acquaintances managed to get over their heartbreak quicker because they *look happier* in the same timeframe that it took you to get in the shower once every three days.

Our biggest problem when we're healing is that the bad days really get to us. For instance, when you're recovering from heart-break and you resort to stalking your ex on social media because you want to know what they're up to, not only can the results make you uncomfortable, but so can your actions. *'How could you do that?'* you tell yourself off. *'I thought you were better than this.' 'After all these months and you're still not over them? I can't believe you.'*

Perhaps you've spent the better part of the last six months read-ing online articles in health and lifestyle magazines that give you advice on how to move on. I know I did. I'd often search things such as, 'What are the various stages of heartbreak?' and 'Why can't I get closure?' to get some answers to the questions that kept rumbling in my mind. So, knowing that your actions above go against every art-icle you've read about moving on can add to the guilt. Especially the prescriptive one you might have read the other day, outlining how the next 12 months will look after your broken relationship, with month six titled 'the month of internal reflection' – the month that you're doing this God-forsaken stalking – and month 12 titled 'give love another chance'.

> When things don't work out, we attach a lot of
> self-blame to ourselves. We feel that
> something is wrong with us and that's why this

happened. We start to believe that we're
unworthy. We don't appreciate that maybe this
was a blessing in disguise. We don't appreciate
that maybe something better is meant for us.

Your exceptional social media stalking skills can bite you in the ass. You assume that others have figured out how to heal from heartbreak, *but you haven't because you're still stalking your ex.* This may make you feel dreadful about yourself. You let yourself drown in self-depleting thoughts and stray further away from self-compassion, which is what you *need*, now more than ever to heal from your heartbreak.

But. But. But.

We now know that healing journeys are not linear; they are staggered, unpredictable and even messy. Now that you understand healing better, you can appreciate that slipping backwards on your path to move on *does not mean* that you've not made any progress at all. Taking a few steps back, missing your ex, scrolling on their social media feed or spending the day crying after a few weeks of easy self-love practices doesn't mean that all those steps you took have been washed away. It means you're human. Because healing is a few steps forward and a few steps back.

Sure, maybe going on a social media stalking spree wasn't one of your brightest moments, but *we've all been there*. Trust me. Many of you may have drunk dialled an ex, many have also turned up at their house, pleading with them to take you back, many have created fake social media profiles and added them as a friend to see what they'd do. We've done it all. We've all carried out actions during the moving on stage that we know, deep down, will cause us pain – but we do them anyway because that's just how feelings work.

Feelings are chaotic and out of your control and sometimes over-take your sanity. But that's okay. It's normal. It isn't the end of the world, I promise, and – if you are – stop treating it as though it is. The moment that you stop seeing healing as a prescriptive, one-size-fits-all approach, you can value the individuality of everyone's experiences and how each of you move on in different ways.

The bottom line is that other people's journeys out of heartbreak, or their perception of your heartbreak, shouldn't deter-mine how you feel, or the pace at which you move forward. Because your journeys can't and shouldn't be compared. So, if Sam down the road found a new man in the time that it took you to start doing your laundry – *that's okay*. Your healing journeys are very personal and as unique as the DNA that you carry.

In this journey, you can have a great week of practising easy self-care, which involves going to a yoga class, catching a movie with a friend and meeting up with your mum for brunch, followed by a few heavy days where even getting out of the bed is difficult and all you can do is scroll through your WhatsApp messages to see what went wrong. What truly happened. Why did it fall apart in the way that it did? Both versions of your story are normal. Both versions are of you healing. They are of you healing.

Sometimes it can be hard to be positive when you're in the trenches of heartbreak, because moving on from someone who you thought was your future isn't easy. In these moments, be patient with yourself. Don't compare your journey to others. Don't engage in self-blame. Be compassionate. Your heart needs it. Your heart needs it.

journal

How would you describe what happened to cause your heartbreak?

Were the circumstances that caused you to fall apart in your control?

What would you have done differently?

What – if anything – have you learned?

If you can't answer all the questions, don't worry, just try your best.

Sometimes it doesn't work out, it just doesn't. No matter how hard you try to glue your pieces together, no matter how hard you try to fix it and no matter how much you talk about the sticky stuff, the painful stuff, the hard, messy, hurts-to-remember stuff, you can't move on from it. You can't forget the hurt that they caused and how lonely they made you feel — every single time that they put you last. You can't forget the expectations you had and how they let you down, time and time again. You can't go back to the gentle, simmering love you had for them when you first met — because now, that feeling has been replaced with disappointment, with regret, with wishing that things hadn't gone this way but knowing that you can't go back in time. Because now, too much has happened and you've both said things that you can't take back. Because now, you've seen a side to them that you never knew existed and they've seen a side to you that you didn't know you had — the mean, cruel side that only they bring about. Sometimes it doesn't work out because you not only bring the best out in each other but the worst too. And the hardest part is knowing that they could have been your forever if only things hadn't gone the way they have. And knowing that even though every particle of you wants to hold on to them, you still let them go — because it <u>wasn't meant to be</u>.

DON'T BLAME YOURSELF FOR THE HEARTBREAK

I hope we're on the same page – pun intended – when I say that healing from heartbreak is hard. It is so, so hard. You feel low on most days and weeks after the relationship breaks off. Getting out of bed becomes a chore. Engaging in basic day-to-day tasks start to drain you. And you end up in this phase where either you walk around the house like a lost zombie, wrapped in a fluffy blanket, a tub of ice cream hidden in the crook of your elbow, or you go out partying every night indefinitely because you want to escape the pain.

But neither choice does anything to ease your discomfort.

After the denial stage is over (where you can't accept that it all ended, and you continue to contact them and try to make things work, until you do/don't receive closure), you start questioning why it didn't work out. You ask yourself whether you could have done things differently. Maybe you shouldn't have made that final call ending the relationship. Maybe you should've stopped them when they told you that they were leaving. Maybe you should've been more patient and believed them when they said, *'We're just friends, she doesn't mean anything to me,'* after you came across another compromising photo of them with someone else.

You should've tried more, understood more, listened more, loved more.

The bottom line is that *you failed*. The relationship is over *because of you* and now you're all alone, and probably will be forever, and it's all your fault.

These self-deprecating thoughts arise from low self-esteem, so the percentage of truth in them is very low. Your relationship wasn't one-sided, so it's illogical to blame only yourself for its downfall. Sure, you could have done things differently, *but they could have too*. You weren't the only one in that relationship and it doesn't make sense to solely carry the guilt of causing them, and yourself, pain.

> *To move on, let your reality be directed by thoughts and beliefs that are grounded in self-compassion.*

But consider that you've shared the guilt evenly. You blame them too. In fact, you carry lots of anger towards them. They could've made more effort. They could've called you more. They could've cut off friends that were a bad influence, and maybe all of this wouldn't have happened. Now it's over, and it's not just your fault – it's their fault too.

Then you turn it back on yourself. *But no,* you think, *it's my fault, because I chose them.* As a result, you start questioning your choice in romantic partners. *Why do I always pick people like this? It's me. It's all me. I'm the one that keeps putting myself in this situation.* Once more, it all comes back to the negative self-talk. Once more, it becomes about everything that you've done wrong, and how this heartbreak is evidence of all your failures. You then feel unworthy. Unlovable. Not enough.

At this point you may realise that these feelings are hinting at something deeper, because how could a single heartbreak make you feel so bad about yourself?

So, let's unpack where these damaging views come from and how to tackle them.

What Does Heartbreak Say about You?

Why do we feel negatively about ourselves when we experience heartbreak? Why do we have low self-esteem?

There are underlying elements to the negative self-talk and low self-worth we may experience following heartbreak. The person who broke your heart didn't suddenly implant these feelings in your mind (unless they were a crappy partner, treated you poorly and talked down to you, in which case they're not worthy of you grieving them), because you already had those beliefs to begin with.

Let me repeat; *you already had negative beliefs about yourself to begin with.*

I acknowledge that there are cases where you have had a nour-ishing childhood and a healthy attachment with your parents, but you still end up with someone who treats you horribly, causing you to question everything about yourself to the point where you no longer feel loved or cared for, despite all the other strong relation-ships in your life.

But most of the time our beliefs about who we are and what we deserve – indeed our entire reality – has a strong foundation in our childhood and early adolescent years.

Let me give you a personal example. Because of my difficult childhood I developed very low self-esteem.

Even though I appeared confident, loud and boisterous as a teenager, I had very low self-worth, and deep down I would've set-tled for the bare minimum in all aspects of my life: my career, my familial relations, my friendships, any romantic relationships and my dreams. Now that I've done the reflective work, and continue to do so, I understand what – and who – I deserve, but this wasn't the case before I experienced heartbreak.

It's for this reason that I can confidently tell you that when I first had my heart broken, the person responsible didn't plant those negative thoughts in my mind, he just made them apparent to me. Those thoughts already existed before him. Elements of my childhood had already given me enough toxic beliefs about my worth to last me a lifetime.

The negative self-talk was there without him having to do a thing.

If the relationship had worked out, we would have been happy together for a few months or years and I would have buried those damaging beliefs in a corner of my mind. But every time that we would argue, or the relationship would get slightly rocky, those feelings would re-emerge, and I would feel horrible about myself all over again, until eventually the relationship would end – which it had to, because my low self-regard meant that my choice in romantic partners wasn't a healthy one – and the debilitating beliefs about myself would reappear, as though they had never left to begin with.

Whenever I'd get my heart broken, it wouldn't *cause* me to have low self-esteem; instead it would *water the seeds* of low self-worth that I carried with me all those years.

When you see heartbreak in this way, you can identify why you might take others leaving you so personally.

It's not that this person was the best thing that could ever have happened to you (maybe they were, but most likely not), or that you missed your chance because you didn't tell them that you loved them sooner. It's about *why* you think they were the best thing to happen to you and not the other way around, or what truly stopped you from expressing your feelings to your best friend of 15 years until it was too late. When you start to rewind and look back at the structures of your childhood, you can learn to acknowledge where your negative self-talk comes from, which is the first step towards trying to change it.

This is an act of tough self-love. Earlier in the book we talked about what tough self-love is: 'Rewinding the reel of your past to pluck out traumatic events that have caused you to have low self-esteem or trust issues . . .'

When you're heartbroken, the most valuable device that you can use is self-love. And not just easy self-love, because going for walks to the park, seeing your girls to offload and watching a few rom-coms with a tub of Ben & Jerry's is great, I agree, *but you need more.* You need tough self-love.

Practising tough self-love will motivate you to not only deal with your current heartbreak but also dig deeper. The deeper you dig, the more steps you will take towards healing from your heartbreak. Doing the challenging work, the kind I mentioned earlier on page 10 (asserting boundaries, giving yourself closure, getting therapy, having difficult conversations, acknowledging your mistakes, letting people go, etc.), will help you find relief from your current pain, and you will also be equipped with tools that prevent you from falling into similar situations in the future. These tools can be anything from a sharp instinct, the ability to deeply reflect on people's actions and words, noticing the red signs sooner, validating yourself, appreciating what you deserve, creating a basic list of healthy qualities that you're looking for in a romantic partner, and more.

Remember that closure is for you, and you only. You can sit down with yourself and close old chapters. You can answer those what-how-why questions that pester you at night. You can challenge the negative self-talk that results from the lack of a goodbye. Closure can happen with you, and you only.

Through practising tough self-love, you will also notice the patterns in your previous romantic relationships. Perhaps your relationships have always been chaotic. You've relied too much on romantic partners for joy and fulfilment. You've looked for stability in your romantic relationships because of the lack of stability in the rest of your life.

By reflecting on your past experiences, you will also start to recognise the pattern in the personalities that you've been attracted to in the past and continue to be attracted to; were they unreliable, clingy, unattached, easily dependable, controlling, soft, loud or commanding?

This will teach you about your beliefs about love and what your ideal partner has looked like until now, both of which are based on your early experiences and your observation of the world around you.

Getting closure, letting people go and setting boundaries is an excellent form of self-love. It means that you're acknowledging where things could have gone wrong, and you're accepting what you truly deserve after a long time of self-neglect. It means you're acting on the self-love declaration in relation to heartbreak, which usually takes the form of, '<u>It didn't end because I wasn't worthy, it ended because I deserve more.</u>' It's the 'more' that you're learning, it's the 'more' that you finally see and manifest into.

Think about your last few romantic partners/potential romantic partners.

What traits of theirs were you attracted to?

What traits of theirs were you not attracted to?

Do the attractive/unattractive traits of these romantic partners overlap?

Can you notice a pattern?

If there was one trait that you wouldn't like your ideal partner to have, what would it be?

Did any of your earlier romantic partners have this trait?

Letting go isn't always about putting the other person in a mental box of 'people I no longer care about' or blocking them on social media and deleting their number. Letting go isn't always about thinking ill of the other person. Sometimes, letting go is forgiving them. Letting go is accepting that they hurt you, but not allowing that hurt to define your entire relationship or cloud your memories of them. Letting go is about understanding that sometimes you can love someone and still be disappointed in them, sometimes you can love someone and still distance yourself from them. Sometimes you can love someone but know that because they didn't treat you well, you have to cut off your ties with them. Sometimes you can love someone but still can't forget what they did to you, and that's why you have to leave. Letting go doesn't always mean having negative feelings towards them by the time the relationship ends. Letting go can also mean wishing them well in all their future chapters but knowing that this last chapter was as far as you both were meant to go together. Letting go means keeping them in your heart forever, and moving forward in your life with that feeling, instead of with them beside you.

HOW TO USE TOUGH SELF-LOVE PRACTICALLY

Years ago, when I was heartbroken, I felt as powerless as when I lost my mum. I was four when my entire childhood was snatched away from me, and I had no control over how scattered my upbringing would be. I had no control over my dad's health, the number of social workers I was assigned to or the child protection plans I was put on. I had no control over the various decisions all the 'responsible' adults in my life would make in 'my interest', without ever asking me what I wanted.

I was thrust into the same story of being powerless when I had my heart broken at 21. I wasn't given a choice to be happy and instead, someone whom I trusted had made the decision for me – it wasn't going to work, and we had to part ways. This triggered me in many ways, and I wouldn't realise it then, but in hindsight the reason why I was so hurt was because I was reminded that I wasn't in control of my life. All the bleak memories of my childhood returned, the ones where I couldn't voice my feelings and was sent from one place to another, my life tumbling around like damp clothes in a dryer. I wanted so badly to get out of this situation, but little did I know that not only would I move on from the pain that I was feeling, but also from the false belief that what I felt for this person was 'love'.

Self-love allowed me to embrace a healthier version of love – in all its romantic and non-romantic shades – that I wouldn't have understood before.

One thing was clear: there was something wrong with my idea of love. But why? Well, let's rewind.

I saw my dad suffer horribly after my mum's death. He treated his undiagnosed PTSD with alcoholism for years, causing himself and those around him pain and refusing to get help. This resulted in me having a very chaotic upbringing, where sometimes I had the dad who made sure we were washed and clean, the dad who spent time with us, cared for us and made us laugh, the dad who took us to school, packed us lunch and cooked us dinner, but a lot of the time I had the dad who was unable to pull himself out of the dark hole that my mum's death had put him in. This dad was lost and intoxicated. He was confused and hurting.

Experiencing all of this for decades led me to this subconscious conclusion: *if love caused you pain, then it was real; if it didn't, it wasn't.* The only bittersweet truth of my life had been that my dad had loved my mum with every fibre of his being. But the most important love story in my life, the one of my parents, hadn't ended well. So, what was love if not pain and suffering? What was love if not hurting, crying and breaking down for the person that you loved?

exercise

Have you ever had an experience that seemed out of your control? Maybe you were made redundant, a friend moved away, your partner broke up with you, you were ghosted or maybe you were left out by friends.

Write this down, and if there are more than one, write each one down on a new page.

Now I want you to consider what you can do about this situation going forward.

Remember, in life there are many things that happen to us that we don't have control over, but what we do have control over is how we move on from them and who we become as a result.

For instance, my mum's death was completely out of my control. It was an event that I could do nothing about, and I let myself feel miserable about it for years afterwards.

Eventually, I transformed my present. I stopped playing the victim card and I started to take back the control that had taken from me. Instead of getting upset over the lack of opportunities I had, I started grabbing every other opportunity that did come my way. **I changed my mindset**. *I noticed the negative thoughts and tried to counter them with something positive. I changed the damaging narrative in my mind into something nourishing, into something that helped me heal.*

For example, instead of thinking, **'I'm not worthy of anything, this is why everything goes wrong,'** *I told myself,* **'Things may not have turned out the best until now, but as long as I keep my head held high, and my loved ones close, I can change the rest of my journey.'**

In the same way, I want you to consider how you can change your mindset, and your story, about this experience going forward. Now, write it down, and turn to this the next time that event bothers you.

Subconsciously, I took this 'truth' about love forward with me. Even though I told myself that I would have a healthy relationship, I had never seen one. I had no positive role models to go by. In fact, the only time I felt *love* for this person was when I was hurting because of him. When things were good, I didn't feel an ounce of romantic love towards him, and this really irked me when I was trying to move on. I asked myself constantly, did I truly love this person? Because if I did, why did I only feel the love when I was hurting?

It took a conversation with my friend, months after the heartbreak, for me to understand that I was *choosing* to hold on to the pain because pain was the only thing that reminded me of love, and because love had been lacking in my life for so long, I didn't want to let go of it. If I let go of the pain, I'd let go of the only feeling of love I'd ever known – and this terrified me. Another reason I kept holding on was because it meant I had some sense of control over my life. Deep down I knew that the moment I let go of this pain I would be powerless once again, because choosing to stay in pain was the only thing I had control over. But it wasn't healthy, it never had been, and if I wanted to be truly happy, then I had to let go of both the hurt that I was feeling as well as the false idea of love that I'd spent so long holding on to.

ASK YOURSELF THE DIFFICULT QUESTIONS

If you're feeling low after a breakup, ask yourself: *'Why do I feel this way?'*

Answering this question means looking back at the cloud of memories of the years before this relationship. Experiences that built you, people who you learned to love from, events that changed you. Look into them. Observe them. Try to understand why you feel the way that you do. Maybe your relationship breakdown made you feel insecure about how you look; can you recall other times in your life when you've felt insecure?

If, for example, you had a long-term friend that you loved but never felt confident enough to tell them – ask yourself why you couldn't bring yourself to confess. What stopped you going through with it? If the answer is something along the lines of 'Because they would say no', 'Because I'm not good enough', or 'Because it would never work, and I would lose my friend', then consider why you have these beliefs. If you had a healthy, thriving friendship with this person, then it's unlikely that it caused you to question your worth. Instead, the reasons why you didn't confess your love are founded upon damaging beliefs about your worth and fear of rejection – beliefs that were likely formed over months and years of your childhood and adolescent life.

journal

How did your heartbreak make you feel about yourself? E.g., it made me question if I'm good enough, it caused me to be uncomfortable in my skin, I'm no longer as confident as I was.

Have there been other moments in your life where you have felt this way? E.g., previous relationship, in my friendship group, on a night out.

When you think of your ex, what kind of emotions come up?

How do you currently feel about moving on from this person?

Be as honest as you can.

Looking back at your past to unpack your feelings so you can move on from your heartbreak is not simple. It requires weeks and months of self-reflection, speaking to your close ones, reading books on the topic, journalling, and even attending courses and getting therapy. But eventually you will find the root cause of why you might have started disliking yourself and begun to engage in negative self-talk after your heart got broken.

Embracing self-love will reveal how easy it is to allow heartbreak to fan the flames of negativity you hold towards yourself. Embracing self-love will show you that all this time, you've been giving this heartbreak the power to fuel your dark and damaging thoughts. Embracing self-love will encourage you to accept yourself as you are, even if someone else couldn't.

> Self-love is truly healing. When you adopt a compassionate perspective towards yourself, you can mend your heart in ways you never knew before, especially after a heartbreak, because feelings of low self-regard need to be tackled with positive thoughts, nourishing self-talk and boundless compassion towards yourself. That is what makes all the difference. That is what will change your journey for good.

WHY AM I WITH A SOUL-SUCKING VAMPIRE?

Often, despite having a healthy, nourishing childhood, you can get into a toxic relationship with a blood-sucking vampire who – instead of nourishing your soul – drinks up all the good in your life. They feed into your insecurities. They make you feel bad about yourself –

whether it's your looks, your goals or your confidence – and they push you into a tight corner that you're unable to escape, even after they're no longer in your life.

It's understandable in these cases to say that the negative self-talk is a result of *them* being in your life and the heartbreak that they caused.

But it's still not that clear cut. Because then you ask yourself why you're with a soul-sucking vampire to begin with. Do they represent someone in your life that you looked up to? Do they represent your inner longing to be a saviour; were they just a project for you to work on? Do you have a deep-seated wish to be a rebel for once, after being seen as a straight-A, rule-abiding, picture-perfect individual for so long?

To search for these answers you must return, once more, to the building blocks of your childhood and early adolescence, and you're left with the potential, once again, that traces of self-doubt existed long before you met this person – they just fuelled them further or validated your own harmful feelings towards yourself.

I want you to remember that looking back and finding the source of your low self-confidence or grim thoughts shouldn't result in self-blame. It shouldn't mean looking at yourself in the mirror and repeating *'It's all your fault because you had no reason to, but you still pick people like this'* or *'It's all your fault because you let what he/she/they did get to you'*. It's not about self-blame. It's about finding the core cause(s) of your aching discomfort once your relationship ends. It's about finding the reason why their leaving might have affected you *so badly* that perhaps you're still unable to move on.

Because sure, everyone's timeline is different, and your healing shouldn't be comparable to someone else's, but you still need to ask yourself – *why does it hurt so much?* You will then discover that it was never about them leaving and always about *you wanting them to stay*, despite all the distress that the relationship brought you both.

Self-love encourages you to change the narrative about your heartbreak in your mind. The moment that you change the story from <u>'They left me because I deserved it'</u> to <u>'I didn't deserve to be treated poorly and they were wrong to treat me like that. I'm still worthy of love,'</u> you will take control of your current situation and transform this healing journey of yours for the better.

exercise

Let's return to the journal prompt you did at the start of this section.

'Have you been through/are you experiencing a heartbreak?'

For those of you who are currently experiencing heartbreak or are on a healing journey, I want you to think of the following pointers:

✳ *When did this heartbreak take place?*

✳ *Have you had closure? If so, how? And if not, why not?*

✳ *How far do you feel you've come?*

✳   *Have you engaged in self-blame? When and why?*

✳   *What qualities of theirs would you look for in your future romantic partner?*

✳   *What qualities of theirs are now a red flag?*

✳   *Write down five self-love practices you can engage in to move on. If you don't have any yet, this is time to set yourself some self-love tasks, e.g., a day of self-care, meet up with a friend, do a social media cleanse, listen to a podcast, go for a run, write down a list of gratefulness.*

✳   *Write down five lessons you can take away from this heartbreak.*

✳   *Do you feel you're confident in knowing what you deserve from a romantic partner? If yes, what is this?*

Some things just aren't meant to be. And I know that it's hard to accept for many of us who dreamed of a future together with the person that we now have to leave behind — but there's no other way out of the situation that you find yourself in than this; <u>you have to leave</u>. They have to go. You both have to accept that this was as far as your journey together was supposed to take you. You have to move on. Sometimes a relationship doesn't work out because you both deserve different things. Sometimes it doesn't work out because you weren't right for them or they weren't right for you. Sometimes it doesn't work out because you both need to heal, grow and become different people — and if the people that you're meant to be are aligned then you will find your way back to each other. Sometimes it doesn't work out because you can't be the best version of yourself with them and they can't be the best version of themselves with you. Whatever the reason, rather than holding each other back, gather the strength to let go. Gather the strength to move on. Only then will you make room for all the wonderful people and adventures that are waiting for you.

chapter 3

healing from emotional abuse

Remember those moments of impact I spoke about at the start of the introduction? The ones that mark the beginnings of healing journeys? Sometimes these moments can be a singular, individual event, and sometimes they're not moments at all. They are months and years of trauma that we try to scrub off like dirt from our skin but are unable to.

Trauma can change your life in unimaginable ways. Facing a traumatic event, several traumatic events or the same event over many years can lower your self-esteem, urge you to question what you deserve and encourage you to engage in self-neglect instead of self-love.

I was seven when I was first called fat by my family member. She didn't say the word 'fat' directly, nor did she sound condescending when she uttered the words that stole the floor from beneath me. Her face was sombre, in fact, a worried line cast across her forehead when she took in what I was wearing, traditional Indian clothes – loose navy-blue embroidered trousers patterned with sequins and a rose-coloured cropped blouse, along with a net dupatta (a long shawl worn to cover your head or shoulders) that my cousin had secured with a safety pin on my shoulder – before sitting me down to have 'a talk'.

My cousin was wearing the same outfit, but in a different colour. It was her mum, my aunt, who bought the matching clothes for us from Southall, a suburban town in greater London with a significant South Asian population, a few days before for a family friend's wedding. She was thrilled when we tried the clothes on upon our return home, her face splitting into a wide grin when we both twirled in our crisp new party outfits.

We always went to Southall to shop for Indian attire, and the outfit I'd worn that day was my absolute favourite. Although I was born in India, I'm actually of Afghan Sikh heritage, a community that not many people are familiar with. But I've never visited Afghanistan myself and only know of the dusty lanes, pointy hills and vast villages through faded photographs and the stories that my dad and aunt have told me. After the Taliban rose to power in the late 1980s, thousands of Hindu and Sikh minorities were forced to leave their homes and flee for their lives. My family, and thousands of others, carved their way by immigrating to the West, including the UK, and now the town of Southall boasts shopping centres, shops and boutiques of all sizes that are run mostly by Afghan Sikh retailers. It's amazing to see how far we've come from where we were.

As a child, I loved visiting Southall. My aunt would take all six of us – four of her children, along with me and my brother – almost every weekend after visiting the Gurudwara, the Sikh temple. I thoroughly enjoyed those days. The streets would be filled with pedestrians, shopping bags in hand as they shuffled in and out of neon-signed shops lining the wide, traffic-clogged street. Bollywood hits would roar from speakers perched in the corners of open-mouthed stalls, the waft of fresh jalebi and pakoras luring us in as we passed. But instead, all us kids would go directly to the sweetcorn stall, warming our hands over the cooker as my aunt bought us £1 hot sweetcorn pots to share.

For over a decade, I spent almost every weekend at my aunt's house and developed a close bond with all her children. As a result, me and my cousin grew up like sisters. We wore the same clothes everywhere we went, and we basked in the compliments we received whenever we'd parade in with our matching dresses, shoes and identical hair-styles, as though we were twins instead of first cousins. I couldn't imagine that there was anything wrong with what we were doing.

That is until a family member enlightened me at the young age of seven.

'Why are you wearing that?' she asked with a serious look in her dusty brown eyes.

'What do you mean?' I frowned, patting down the fabric with my hands.

Her eyes flickered over me once.

'This cropped blouse doesn't suit you.'

I was confused. My cousin was wearing the same outfit. 'Why not?' I asked.

'Because . . .' Disbelief clouded her face at my cheek to ask such a question. 'Your cousin is beautiful,' she went on. 'She's fair, skinny and can wear anything . . .' She paused, giving thought to her next few words. 'I'm sorry, Ruby, but you're a little overweight. This type of outfit doesn't suit girls that look like you. I'm only trying to help,' she added, softening the blow.

But my self-esteem was already shattered.

Do you have memories of being criticised as a child? How did this make you feel?

When did you start noticing your body shape?

What kind of message did you receive from family, friends or society about your body?

HOW BODY-SHAMING AFFECTS YOUR SELF-ESTEEM

Conversations like this became more frequent after I turned seven, or perhaps they were always common but it wasn't until then that I could finally process what was being said to me. Whenever my family got together, my cousins would joke about my weight. Mentioning the food on my plate was a part of their regular chitchat, as though they were talking about the weather rather than what a young girl was eating.

The moment we would sit down for dinner, a traditional Afghan tablecloth spread out across the floor, flanked by mattresses and cushions, with an array of salads, yogurt, chicken, rice, fritters, naan and dal spread out evenly across the large space, the digs would start. They would say things like, 'Ruby, isn't that too many pakoras? Leave some for the others,' or, 'Who wants ice cream? Not you, Ruby, you've already had enough to eat. You don't want to get fat, do you?' before noticing the fallen expression on my face and correcting themselves. 'Go on, then. You won't get fat,' they'd chuckle.

My extended family constantly compared me to my skinnier, fairer cousin, the one I loved as a sister, and they often took turns at making jabs, turning my appearance into the focal point of all their humour. I was also the butt of all jokes because of my excessive facial hair (a blessing from my South Asian heritage), and the colour of my skin. I was darker than my cousin, that much was clear. But my family never failed to point this out to me, as though I would forget if they didn't vocalise it often.

The worst part is I don't think they realised what they were doing. They were *just having a laugh*. They didn't know what their words were doing to me, and, frankly, I didn't know either until years later.

But regardless, I spent my entire childhood hearing such negative words about my weight and appearance. There wasn't a week when my round cheeks weren't squeezed with an exaggerated, 'Aww, you are so cute,' or questions about my weight weren't tossed back and forth across the dinner table like a game of tennis.

Being a parent, my dad felt bad seeing me being spoken about in this way. He felt sorry for me. He started to overcompensate at home. He bought me takeaways every weekend and cooked mouth-watering (but heavily fried) food, all the while reassuring me that I was 'not fat and should eat more'. But my brother responded differently. He thought that the only way to shut everyone up would be by *changing* me. Even when I was as young as eight, he would take me running around the park on the weekends. Sometimes he joined me on the field and other times he would ride his bike and urge me to run after him – just like those TV shows about 'fat camps' where heavily overweight people are pushed beyond their comfort zone to lose weight.

My brother always said, 'Lose weight so that no one makes fun of you.' His belief, and the belief of many of us who have been made to feel like this, was that if the world treats you a certain way, you should change yourself rather than those around you. He was a child, and he didn't know any better. **But we do**.

While both these men in my life – in their own obscure way – did their best to make me feel better, their actions did the opposite. *I felt so, so much worse.*

> Emotional abuse is a form of chronic trauma –
> an experience that happens consistently over
> a prolonged period – and it has a devastating
> effect on your self-worth and self-esteem.

I shouldn't have to, but I'm conditioned by society and all the experiences of my nearly 30 years to clarify that *I was never overweight*. I can show you a childhood photo to prove it (again, I shouldn't have to). I was short and on the chubby side, but it was the kind of childhood chub that melts away when you enter adolescence. Or at least it would have if it wasn't for the unhealthy relationship with food that I eventually developed.

No culture is without its faults and South Asian culture, in particular, is known for fat-shaming and colourism. For decades, some of the bestselling skincare products in countries such as India have been aimed at dark-skinned brown women who are reminded daily by society about how desirable fair skin is.

Do these skin-lightening products work? Absolutely not.

But do they profit off the insecurities of marginalised brown women? Yes, sir!

Looking further into history will tell us that colourism and fat-shaming are norms that have been perpetuated by Western ideology, colonisation and widespread media, but let's not talk about historical blame for a second and instead focus on the topic at hand.

After being criticised for my weight over the years, I became extremely self-conscious. I developed low self-esteem and I had this feeling that always lingered at the back of my mind, one that told me that I was never good enough. This bled into my adulthood, affecting my self-confidence when it came to my personal and inter-personal relationships.

It was only when I began my healing journey and adopted self-love that I recognised how harmful those words had been, and I noticed the toxic relationship patterns in my life that were a result of those early experiences.

The form of fat-shaming that consumed my childhood is an example of emotional abuse, which is one type of trauma that you can experience, and trauma – as you've seen already – starts new healing journeys. But before I dive into the rest of my story, I want to make sure that we're both aligned when I say 'emotional abuse'.

Emotional abuse is damaging for your mental, emotional and physical health and well-being, and a lot of the time the ill-treatment is from the people who are close to you. For this reason, it's difficult to recognise it – because you don't think that the people who love you have the heart to harm you.

When was the last time you felt bad about yourself?

What happened? Who was involved?

Before this feeling, did you have any interaction with other people that caused feelings of discomfort?

Would you say that the negative feelings you had about yourself were in some way linked to the behaviour of others, or was it internal?

Are You Being Emotionally Abused?

With emotional abuse, the victim often doesn't have a clue what they've gone through until many years down the line when they begin to reflect. And regardless of whether you have or haven't experienced emotional abuse, the tips and life skills shared in this section can support you in other healing journeys and areas of your life where you're facing challenges – so, please continue reading.

People who experience emotional abuse, either in their childhood, adolescence or adulthood, have a diminished sense of self. They don't regard themselves highly, they engage in harmful self-talk and often they look to their emotional abusers for validation.

I want to clarify that even if someone exhibits toxic or abusive behaviour, it doesn't mean that they will be labelled a 'bad' person in society. Sometimes people can act in toxic ways without knowing that their behaviour is toxic. And sometimes people with toxic or negative traits engage in normal daily life, have mostly healthy relationships and can be seen as 'good people'. For example, maybe you have a manager who constantly criticises your work, is controlling and passive aggressive and subtly belittles you in front of your team, but they're seen by most as a 'great person with a beautiful family'. Maybe your parents, who always set such high standards for you, never compliment your achievements, but don't fail to point out when you let them down. You wouldn't – at least not always – call your parents horrible human beings or 'bad people', but perhaps they just need to unlearn the problematic parental models they picked up from their own respective upbringings.

This isn't the case in *all* instances of emotional abuse, and emotional abusers can be threatening, aggressive and dangerous, as well as verbally and even physically abusive. But sometimes you can be emotionally abused by someone without you realising it, and this will contribute to your feelings of low self-esteem and increased reliance on them for your emotional needs.

> The need to heal from emotional abuse and ill-treatment is the calling that you receive from your innermost part to treat yourself better. To love yourself. To live a life that brings you joy and peace.

Strong Emotional Abuse vs Subtle Emotional Abuse
It's helpful to distinguish between cases of **strong emotional abuse**, such as violent and threatening behaviour, financial isolation, blackmail, bullying and domestic abuse, and **subtle emotional abuse**, such as humiliation, constant criticism, power-play, being made fun of, passive aggression and controlling behaviour. By 'subtle' I don't mean that the emotional abuse is less damaging to you, but that it's not necessarily easily recognisable as abuse. When you experience subtle emotional abuse, you're more likely to let yourself continue to be controlled and you stay in those relationships without realising what they are doing to your self-esteem.

RECOGNISING EMOTIONAL ABUSE

Emotional abuse is an example of chronic trauma; experiencing something damaging over an extended period of time. Other examples include domestic abuse, difficult family dynamics, a toxic relationship or bullying.

When you're thinking about emotional abuse, it's important to consider certain signs that can indicate whether you are or have observed someone in an emotionally abusive relationship (both personal and professional):

* *Rejection – your thoughts, feelings and opinions are never accepted, e.g., parents who point out everything you do wrong and never congratulate you on your achievements. This is subtle emotional abuse.*

* *Negative talk – they are rude, talk down on you, are passive aggressive and even shout and swear at you, e.g., a boss who makes you feel anxious and afraid, and you're walking on eggshells because nothing you do seems to please them. This can be both subtle and strong emotional abuse.*

* *Humiliation – they constantly criticise you, make fun of you, treat you badly and disrespect you in social situations. This is strong emotional abuse.*

* *Gaslighting – they manipulate you into questioning your own credibility, e.g., a friend who questions your every decision. This is strong emotional abuse.*

* *Control – they isolate you from your loved ones, they don't let you do what you want to, you feel obligated to seek permission, e.g., having a toxic romantic relationship with someone who does all of the above. This is strong emotional abuse.*

Maybe you've experienced this in the past and you've long since left those people – but the aftermath of their harmful behaviour still lingers, affecting the way that you think about yourself. Whatever it is, months and years of going through the same emotional roller-coaster can leave you feeling weak and insecure.

Emotional abuse can make you change how you think about yourself. You rely on other people for guidance and affirmation, and you let them control the dynamics of the relationship. You even begin to speak to yourself in the same belittling manner, and worse – you stop loving yourself entirely.

Emotional abuse is very destructive to your well-being, and until you acknowledge what you're experiencing and make the decision to leave or fix the situation, which the path to self-love encourages, you will be stuck there – and in similar situations – forever.

> *When you're healing from trauma, you need to go to war with the negative mindset you've developed using self-love.*

exercise

Based on the signs highlighted above, have you experienced emotional abuse?

✳ *Have you experienced any of the signs of emotional abuse in your relationships, employment or another situation?*

✳ *How does this person make you feel?*

✳ *Have you tried standing up for yourself? If not, what is stopping you?*

✳ *Is there anything you can do? E.g., apply for a new job, speak to them.*

✳ *Has this experience effected any other areas of your life?*

✳ *What is your main goal in healing from this? E.g., I want to be confident again, I want to be comfortable in my weight, I want to break off this relationship, etc.*

HOW HARMFUL IS EMOTIONAL ABUSE?

Being fat-shamed my entire childhood had a detrimental effect on my self-confidence. After being criticised for my weight over the years, I became anxious about what I ate and self-conscious about how I looked. As a 12-year-old, I'd pull my T-shirt over my jeans or pinch the fabric with my thumb and index finger to loosen it so that it wouldn't cling to my body. I refused all offers of chocolate chip cookies – my absolute favourite – and opted for 'healthy' food at school. I never wore sleeveless tops because of my 'big arms' and I wouldn't be caught dead in a skirt, for fear that people would notice my 'hairy legs'.

But when I returned home, I indulged in all the food that I avoided during the day. And once I was done, I felt even worse than I had before. Words of disapproval from everyone would buzz in my mind like bees, giving me as much of a physical headache as an emotional one.

We all know how this story goes, the cycle of feeling low, binge eating, being momentarily joyful and then feeling even worse than before that millions of children and teenagers experience around the world.

Thankfully for me – and I say this with humility – I didn't develop an eating disorder, but I did develop a comfort-eating habit that stayed with me until my early twenties. The physical and mental strain of putting my mind and body through this chaotic relationship with food contributed to my feelings of low self-worth.

To every other person, I looked like an average-sized 18-year-old girl. But the mental and emotional rollercoaster that I went on because of my unhealthy eating habit told a different story altogether.

> The harmful effects of emotional abuse aren't always visible. Sometimes it's in the way that we talk about ourselves. Sometimes it's in the way that we think about ourselves. Sometimes it's in the way that we live our day-to-day lives, hiding, fragile, looking to others for all the answers that we can't find within our own hearts. Emotional abuse is most damaging to our reality. To how we think and how we feel. To who we are and who we become.

One reason emotional abuse continues for so long is because of the control that the abuser has on you, with their words changing your mindset towards yourself. In my case, this was a group of people who thought that they were speaking in my favour, people who believed that by constantly picking at my appearance, they could show me that there was something wrong with the way that I looked – comparatively to my cousin and the poisonous beauty standards implemented by our culture – and encourage me to change it. Some of them didn't even have an intention – without labelling them *cruel*, they just wanted to have a laugh. But no one thought that years of hearing criticism would result in me craving the validation of others, which was reflected in most of the relationships that I formed after.

As a teenager I was attracted to friendships with people I thought were prettier than me, overconfident girls whose one compliment would raise my self-esteem. I craved their attention and being a part of their group made me feel more desirable and attractive. When I talked to boys, I was more attracted to those whose adulation I longed for, the boys who gave me little attention and strung me on long enough to keep me hooked, until I learned what I was doing.

This went on for years until I recognised the unhealthy dynamics that existed in those interactions, when I actively sought to practise self-love and heal from years of emotional abuse.

> Honestly telling someone you love that a colour doesn't suit them once is different to constantly reminding them that they are dark-skinned — comparatively — and shouldn't wear a particular colour. It's not what you say but it's how you say it that makes all the difference.

People say that I've changed, as though it's an insult. As though me no longer swallowing my tongue whole until I choke on my emotions is wrong — because my words, no matter how honest or raw, 'shouldn't hurt others'. As though being half a person — because the whole of me would be 'too much' — is the only way that I should be. Because any more than that would overwhelm those who live by limits. Because any more would mean I would outshine others, as though that somehow justifies putting me in a box rather than urging them to step out of theirs. People say that I've changed as though it is an insult. As though compressing my heart into a fickle seed so it could fit into the palms of those who had no room was how I should have lived forever. But I didn't — couldn't — shouldn't have to swallow my worth any longer. So, I stopped. I stopped bending, moulding and limiting myself to the expectations people had of me and I stood up tall — raised my shoulders — held my head high and refused to lower my gaze. I stopped being a pushover — a doormat — a sling through which people could shoot their shot. People say that I've changed as though it is an insult — as though giving yourself the same respect that you give to others were a crime.

Because of my need for external validation, I changed myself to fit in with the ideal that everyone had set for me. I went through a 'makeover'. I got my legs waxed as young as 16, had my eyebrows done at 15. I ran on the treadmill every summer from the age of 16, because that's when I had the freest time, and I lost all those 'extra' kilograms to become thinner. Basically, all my baby fat. I changed my hairstyle, started box-dyeing my hair and slowly replaced all my clothes with more fashionable alternatives. I still covered myself up because I hadn't become more confident, as my self-confidence depended on the reaction I got from others.

I told myself that this change was a result of me tumbling through the years as a teenage girl does, but deep down it was because I longed for validation. I wanted the people around me to notice this new look and compliment me, and their affirming words would contribute to the worth that I attached to myself.

But what happened next was unexpected. I no longer heard 'Ruby, eat less', but instead I was bombarded by anyone who had ever called me fat now telling me that I looked 'too thin', and I had 'gotten too weak' and that I 'needed to eat something'. It's so ironic. Because it was no longer 'little chubby Ruby'. Now, Ruby's face looked 'too skeletal', and Ruby had 'lost all her glow', and Ruby needed to 'eat something and stop starving herself'.

Brown aunties galore. Need I say more?

In a way, I'm glad that the response I received was the opposite of what I expected. Because imagine everyone said, 'Ruby, you look so amazing' or 'Wow, Ruby. You are stunning!' Then what? This would further fuel my excitement to continue the journey that I was on just because other people approved. I wouldn't have worked on me for me but for what others thought, and *I did need to work on myself.* My toxic relationship with food needed to be fixed (even if it was a result of years of emotional abuse), but this work had to happen independently of the world.

At the end of it, what mattered was *what I thought of myself.*

When I started walking on the path to self-love, I made a mental note to stop letting other people's words bring me down or boost me up. I had to focus on myself and what I needed. This came with a lot of self-love work, work that you must carry out too.

> Growth is a part of life, and we all experience it. So if you've experienced change, then that's normal — but if that change happened because you wanted to prove something, or it came as a result of what someone else said, then ask yourself whether you changed <u>for you or for them</u>.

How Do You Move On from Emotional Abuse?

The first step to take is to acknowledge not only what you experienced but also the damage that this experience has done to your mental and emotional health. The difficult blow that comes with this step is admitting that the people you love have the potential to treat you badly. For me this was admitting that my extended family, the ones who had taken me and my brother in after my mum died and supported my dad in our upbringing, had acted in a way that harmed my self-worth, and it was very tough for me.

How could this be? How could I align the view that I had of them as my saviours with the fact that they were the reason I had body-image issues?

Could the saint and the sinner be the same? *Yes. Yes, they can.*

This is a challenge that you will also face.

Admitting to yourself that your colleagues or loved ones can be awful to you will make them look like the main villain in your story. And while most of the time they are aggressors or bullies – particularly in cases of strong emotional abuse – in a lot of cases they aren't the main villain so much as they are a *lesson*. A lesson that teaches you that your worth doesn't lie in the hands of others. A lesson that highlights how important it is that you draw boundaries so that others can't cross them.

This doesn't take away their accountability for treating you badly. But would you be surprised if I told you that most of the time, people *will not* take responsibility for the way that they've treated you? In fact, a core trait of emotional abusers is their sheer ignorance or rejection of blame regarding their actions. That's why they are such good manipulators and bullies. That's why it's so easy for them to control your mind and your emotions. This is an unfortunate truth of life, a truth that became the driving point for why I began to turn to myself for love and validation.

It's likely that the person who's treated you like this will never apologise or even admit that they've done you wrong. *I know. Ouch.*

So, what happens when you experience emotional abuse, but that person won't accept it, let alone do something about it?

Well, *you do something about it instead* . . .

I think one of the central problems with people in general is our belief that others will eventually live up to the expectations that we have of them. And although a lot of the time they do, this isn't always the case. Not everyone is going to change and become a better person for you. Not everyone is going to realise that they did you wrong and apologise — <u>truly apologise</u> — for the hurt that they caused. Some people just don't change. And as harsh as it sounds, as much as it pains you to hear it, as much as it breaks your heart, it's something you have to accept. Because accepting this will still do you less harm than continuing to wait for those you love to treat you right. Accepting this will still do you less harm than the constant disappointment that washes over you every time they let you down. Accepting this will do you less harm than the harm you're doing to yourself by keeping those who just don't value you in your life. Some people just don't change. So, change your environment instead. Change how lenient you are with them instead. Stop letting them take you for granted and become stronger instead. And change the part of you that gives them power instead. Change the part of you that gives them power instead.

IS THE RELATIONSHIP WORTH SAVING?

Once you recognise that you've experienced – or are experiencing – emotional abuse, ask yourself what steps you want to take going forward. In your healing journey, self-love requires that you prioritise your mental, emotional and physical health through both tough and easy self-love practices. This involves removing anyone and anything that could be harmful to those three things. But one form of self-love is having healthy and honest relationships with others (more on this later).

So, ask yourself – is this relationship redeemable? Can it become a healthy and honest one, or will you have to remove this person from your life entirely because your self-love journey – which is essential to heal from this experience – requires it? If it's redeemable, this will mean getting the relationship to what it needs to be, and this can be done through tough self-love practices.

In cases of strong emotional abuse, I don't recommend redeeming your relationship at all. An abuser in strong cases won't want redemption or even know what redemption is. Even if they promise you that they will change, it's highly likely that weeks and months later you will both slowly slip back, as though you're sinking into quicksand, into your previous roles of abuser and victim. The issue with strong emotional abuse is that the abuse is too substantial and the affect too harmful, and the only way to heal from it is to remove that person from your life and start all over.

Sure, when it comes to colleagues, friends and romantic partners, this may be achievable, but when it comes to family – parents in particular – it is easier said than done. But remember, you don't need to do this on your own. A strong support system, good friends, the useful lessons in this book and others, as well as access to counselling or therapy, can really prove valuable during this time.

In cases of subtle emotional abuse, redemption is possible, and sometimes essential, because you need this person to live a happy and fulfilling life (e.g., a parent, sibling or romantic partner) and redeeming this relationship is an act of self-love. The person who treated you this way might not be a bad person, just highly ignorant of what they're doing, with a habit of perpetuating the same damaging behaviour that they learned in their childhood.

When it comes to parents, this is known as intergenerational trauma; it goes on and on until you recognise it and make a deliberate effort to stop it in its tracks.

> Intergenerational trauma, simply put, is the passing on of historical trauma. For instance, if your grandparents grew up in a war-torn country and prioritised survival tactics over emotional needs, this was then passed over to your parents, who may focus on practical matters and struggle with expressing emotions, saying basic things like '<u>I love you</u>' and empathising with their children.

Redemption can happen in a few ways. Here is just one example of a process that you could follow:

1. *Talk about the prolonged abuse (this can be – but isn't limited to – with your abuser).*
2. *Change your negative patterns of thought/your narrative.*
3. *Take back your power.*

You don't need to follow this as a step-by-step guide; any one of these three points could take longer than others and you don't want to restrict yourself by getting stuck on one step. For instance, as a person of colour and a child of immigrant parents, I can already tell you how daunting number 1 is . . .

TALK ABOUT THE ABUSE

Some of you will find this conversation easier than others, but many will have the following thought: how do you talk about emotional abuse with parents who grew up in war-torn countries where the most important factor in living a steady life wasn't emotional stability but having enough food on the table? Parents who ran away from homes that they built from the ground up and who still view 'mental health' as a whimsical concept that their 1.5/2nd generation children use to come to terms with their multi-identity crisis.

My own dad, who spent his entire childhood and adolescence in Afghanistan, fled his home country as a minority in the late 1990s after the Taliban rose to power. He then faced homelessness and poverty in India, before embarking on a tough and tedious journey to the UK without the rest of his family and losing his beloved wife within a year. None of this was easy. The trauma of leaving your home, having to start all over again, then losing the love of your life and being left with two small children would be enough to ground anyone. For that person, the most important thing to live isn't 'mental stability' but the need to make it through one more day, which makes sense.

With the journey that many of our parents have taken also comes a sense of entitlement. How do you talk about emotional abuse to parents who believe that they have bestowed you with the greatest gift by saving you (even though you weren't even born yet) when they migrated to the West? I say this with as little bitterness or resentment as possible. I, along with all my 1.5/2nd generation friends, am grateful to my dad for the opportunities that I've had because of the fortune of growing up in the West. After all, I probably wouldn't be as privileged as I am today – sitting in a dim-lit café, with a sweet, buttery latte to my right and the sun setting outside as I work on this book – if my family hadn't emigrated.

But none of this should be at the cost of my mental and emotional health.

So, I know it isn't easy. But one way in which I suggest problem-solving this is by *taking it slow*. This means working over months and years on your relationship with your parents/family as opposed to trying to 'fix' it instantly. In that time you can gently introduce conversations about the trauma and emotional abuse that spanned your childhood.

As decades have passed since many of our parents migrated, we can give them the benefit of doubt. I myself have come a long way with my dad in terms of accountability – and although I don't think we will ever get to that point where he will say 'I'm sorry', which I've come to accept, we have reached a point where he acknowledges the negative effect of his actions on my life, and for me that's enough. Because for my journey of healing from childhood trauma, I don't need my family to validate the wrongness of their actions – getting that validation or that apology is just a cherry on the cake of healing that I will eat.

Remember, for your healing, you need to understand what happened, how it negatively affected your well-being and how you can now utilise the tools you've gathered – with self-love being a primary one – to move on.

Similarly, if you can have that conversation about the emotional abuse that you experienced, then that's great. But if you can't, if you find it difficult to bring up that sensitive topic, or it hurts too much, or you're certain that they won't acknowledge their part, then you find other ways of getting the weight off your chest which this conversation would have allowed you to do. Write about it in a journal, talk about it to your friends/loved ones (those who will listen), engage with your support circle, get a therapist if you must – just get it off your chest.

Then take back your power. You know, the power that you handed over to your abuser over the months or years of their abuse. This could be the power to decide what you do, where you go, the personal battles you fight, the friends you make, what you eat and wear, the life choices you make and – most importantly – how you *feel* about yourself.

exercise

Set yourself the task this week to talk about your emotional abuse. Whether it's to a friend, family member, someone you trust, a therapist, just to yourself or even to your abuser – speak about it and let it out of your system.

CHANGE YOUR NARRATIVE

Thoughts are *so important* when it comes to self-love, and self-love is the *key* to our healing.

Months or even years of emotional abuse can result in you forming destructive narratives about yourself – narratives that your emotional abuser has planted in your mind. Most of these are regarding whether you're 'good enough', for a number of things, as well as how incapable you are of functioning without that person. Part of taking back your power from your emotional abuser means pouring it inward.

When I went through the many years of my 'makeover', the main motivating factor was the way that others would react. We all know that this backfired – but this was better for me in the long run. From that point onwards, I took back the power of validation from people who – for so long – had been leeching off my self-worth. I continued working out, eating well, as well as what *I wanted to eat*, and dressing the way I liked without seeking compliments from anyone.

To begin with, because I was so used to not receiving compliments without seeking them, I was taken aback when my friends complimented me. I would lose my train of thought or stop midsentence to process that something nice had been said to me and I hadn't worked hard for it or even anticipated it.

It took time for me to change my belief that someone else's compliments, or lack of them, equalled a *truth* about me. It took me years to understand that others calling me overweight didn't make me overweight, in the same way that them calling me beautiful didn't make me beautiful. I was beautiful if I felt beautiful. I was slim if I felt slim, and I was unhealthy if I felt unhealthy. But remember that diet and physical health isn't the only thing that makes you unhealthy – it has a lot to do with what you consume mentally and emotionally too.

All those truths were related to *my thoughts* about my reality, rather than other people's. Ensuring that these thoughts were healthy, wholesome and reflected an authentic reality took years of self-discovery.

It's important to develop an honest yet nurturing narrative about who you are and love yourself so that you can heal.

Maybe the emotional abuse of many years has resulted in you thinking that you can't do anything without your mother's approval, or that you suck at your job and need your manager's consent to carry out the most menial tasks, or that you should stick with your best friend because she's *the only one* who looks out for you. This is the case when you have a best friend who isolates you from your other friends by constantly telling you false stories – a power-play to make you rely on her, and her only.

Well, now is the time to strip away those narratives and create new ones.

One way to do this is to change the way that you talk to yourself. Instead of saying, 'I need Mum's opinion on this dress before I buy it,' ask yourself, 'Even if Mum doesn't like the dress, do I feel good when I wear it?' If yes, then buy it and tell her about it after. And make sure you don't let her talk you into returning it!

Instead of believing, 'I can't do this presentation until my manager tells me exactly what to write,' remind yourself, 'I've been working in this company for X number of years, so I'm confident that I know what the client is looking for. But if there are any concerns, then I will get a second opinion from a trusted colleague, or potentially my manager.' Instead of letting the thought 'Without my best friend, I won't have a good time' fester, recall how much fun you usually have with the group of girls you go out with, and tell yourself, 'Even if Nisha doesn't come, I'm confident that I will have a great time.'

Write down three examples where you have relied on someone for something that you can do yourself, e.g., 'I relied on my best friend to come shopping with me because I need her opinion on what dress to buy.'

How could you have changed this situation around? E.g., 'I could have trusted my own opinion on the dress and shown my best friend when I got back.'

TAKE BACK YOUR POWER

And finally, you stop letting people treat you a certain way *just because they can*, and you remind yourself that other people's treatment of you does not reflect your worth. You take back your power by drawing boundaries. Boundaries are an incredibly important tool in the realm of self-love, so I've dedicated an entire chapter to them, but for the purpose of this section, here's all you need to know: *a boundary is a line that you draw for your own well-being, implicitly or explicitly, that someone else can't cross.* Boundaries are essential in keeping healthy relationships and can be used to redeem fractured ones.

By now you may have had a conversation (with your abuser, someone you trust or with yourself) about the emotional abuse you experienced, and you have re-examined whether you want this person in your life or not. You then decide to ensure that this doesn't happen again – both with the same person and with someone new – and you do this by changing your narrative. One way you can change the narrative is through the way that you talk to yourself, and the second is through *the way that you speak to others*.

Instead of emailing your manager, 'Is this presentation okay for the meeting?' tell them, 'I've done all the necessary work required to make this presentation professional and agreeable, but if there are any factual errors, please let me know.' Instead of asking your friend, 'Please come out with me and the girls, I won't have a good time without you,' tell her, 'I'm going out with the girls, would you like to come?' Instead of asking your partner, 'Should I apply for this job?' tell them, 'I'm thinking of applying to this job. Let's discuss it over dinner today.'

At face value, these are small variations of the same conversation – but they don't mean the same thing. Changing the way that you speak to someone allows you to form subtle boundaries that they can't cross. Because it's no longer about them judging your work but about them being given a chance to read it, it's no longer about them directing your social life but about them being fortunate enough to be a part of it, it's no longer about your partner deciding what job you can take up but about you valuing them enough to discuss important life decisions with them. It's no longer about your mother deciding what you can wear, eat or do in your life but about you loving her enough to appreciate that she cares while taking the necessary steps to make sure that her care doesn't overstep your own wishes to live your life how you want.

*For the next month, I want you to change the way that you speak to others and take back the power that you have given them. E.g., if you want to go out for a walk, don't tell your partner, 'I can't go without you. Please come with me.' Instead, invite them to come with you and if they decline your invitation, **go anyway**. If you want to take annual leave and have a reasonable amount of time to take it in, don't ask your manager, 'Is it okay if I take this week off?' tell them, 'I'm going away XYZ week and I've requested the leave on the system. Please have a look when you have some spare time.'*

SELF-LOVE IS WHAT MOVES YOU TO PUT YOURSELF FIRST

The decision to end a relationship or not all comes down to self-love. You need to ask yourself why you want to move away from this person who has treated you badly for a long time. Why do you think that this relationship isn't good for you? Why do you feel that your current role isn't the one for you?

Maybe because it's affected your physical health, or it's caused you to lose sleep at night? Maybe you're no longer as confident or outgoing as you used to be, and you'd like to change that? Or maybe you don't feel the same 'love' in your relationship anymore? But no matter how many answers you give yourself, it will always come down to this – the emotional abuse has affected your well-being and now you want to take care of yourself. Now you want to put yourself first.

It all comes down to wanting something better for yourself; the desire to improve your life, the desire to live happily, the desire to be the best version of yourself, the desire to heal and move on.

It won't seem like it right now, and for the longest time I wasn't able to see the picture clearly either – but the longing to take better care of yourself is what empowers you to make those hard decisions. It empowers you to acknowledge that you've been abused, and then to decide whether to leave or to stay and redeem the relationship.

This need to love yourself in the most wholesome way is what pushes you to manifest the best possible environment for you to flourish in.

Emotional abuse can take a lot out of you, but the deep desire to heal and move on can pour so much back in. At the end of the day, your experiences teach you more than they take from you, and it's from the direst situations that you learn to find the light within yourself. That you learn how to save yourself.

In making amends with someone who has – unintentionally – caused you hurt over the last few months and years, do the following, as many times as you can.

1. *Talk about the abuse.*
2. *Change the narrative.*
3. *Take back your power.*

Alternatively, if the above doesn't work, gather the strength to pick up your things – figuratively – and move on.

Forgiveness isn't about letting someone 'off the hook' or condoning their actions. Forgiveness isn't about the world thinking that this person was right all along, and you were wrong, or that they shouldn't regret what they did, or how much they hurt you. Forgiveness isn't about letting them get away with it but about letting <u>you get away from it</u>. Forgiveness is about getting rid of the darkness that's inside your own heart for this person. It's about finally accepting what happened. When you forgive someone, you lift the biting weight of your own resentment towards them and let it go. When you forgive someone, you take away their power — they can no longer affect you, or trouble you, or control your emotions. When you forgive, you accept that even though you don't have the power to change the past, you have the power to leave those who have done you wrong in the past and move on for good. When you forgive, you choose your own happiness over the pain that has had a hold over you for so long. Forgiveness is about choosing yourself and putting your own healing first. It's about letting yourself off the hook from hurting and moving on for yourself, and no one else.

chapter 4

healing from the loss of a loved one

The one thing that is guaranteed in life is death.

A bleak way to start a chapter, I know, but it's true.

This chapter is a testament to this. Some of you might not have experienced heartbreak or emotional abuse (although this is highly unlikely, as these human experiences are common), but every one of you will face the loss of a loved one at some point in your life: *because none of us will live forever.* Everything is temporary. Everyone is temporary. A long life is promised to many of us, but a forever life is promised to none.

And the most beautifully tragic part of losing people, is **knowing that you will lose them**, but not being afraid to love them anyway.

As humans we are social animals, born to love and care for each other. And while many of us understand this, engaging in healthy relationships and prioritising those who pour so much of themselves into us, many of us don't, and end up living empty, hollow lives because we're afraid to let people in.

But that's not what I want for you.

I want you to see all the fluorescent shades of love, loss and pain. I want you to give new people a chance and let those who weren't meant to stay go. I want you to adventure, laugh, cry and enjoy the comfort of tender relationships, because that is what makes life worthwhile.

That is what makes life, *life*.

> Losing someone to an event as serious as death is a type of trauma, and often — depending on how adverse your experiences after this loss are — it's seen as complex trauma because of the variety of emotions, feelings and events that can take place afterwards.

WHO WILL BE THERE FOR YOU NOW?

But sometimes life is hard, especially when you lose someone close to you. Although this chapter uses death as an example, it's still relatable if you've lost a loved one through circumstances that were in or out of your control and they are alive, but you are grieving this loss.

Grief arises after a plethora of experiences. Whether it's death, divorce or a broken friendship or relationship, you can find yourself grieving who you were, the life you wished for or the people that you've lost.

Life is tumultuous, that's a given, and sometimes it can really take a toll on you – particularly when you lose someone that you couldn't imagine your life without, and now you have to live without them. And *it's so, so hard*. Especially in the beginning, when you have one of the bad days. The days that are filled with dark thoughts that cut through your chest: that you will never be okay again, that you're going to be alone forever, that it hurts *so, so much*. The drowning thought that life will never be the same now that they aren't here.

Because who will listen to your stories or laugh at your jokes?

Who will smile at you from across the room or make your favourite dessert?

Who will go on long walks with you, or pick up the phone at 3am when you need them?

Who will be there for you? Who will love you?

> After you lose someone, dark thoughts stab through your mind, reaching your heart in the process. It's a difficult time and you feel yourself drowning in your thoughts. But please, in moments like this, hold on. Please, look for the light at the end of the tunnel. Please, keep walking towards it. There is a way out. There is a way out.

When I experienced grief for the first time, I was four, at an age where I had no idea what grief even was. It's hard to know how grief works for young children, but the simplest way I can describe the feeling is this: something was there before, and after my mum passed away, that something was missing. And that something was **huge**. The lack of it was noticeable in every area of my life.

What made it worse, and I hope that this isn't the case for you if you've lost a loved one, is that my life took a grave hit and the experiences I had after my mum's death were complicated and unfortunate. There was a high turnover of social workers; because we were immigrants, we were shifted from house to house so there was no stability; and my dad's addiction to alcohol had spiralled out of control, to such an extent that I spent much of my childhood in hospital wards by his side while kids my age were doing kid things such as going to the park and playing on swings.

I spent my entire childhood with the fear in the back of my mind that just like my mum, I would lose my dad too. To be honest, as a child of someone with a debilitating lifelong addiction, I will always have that fear, but I no longer give this fear the power to control my happiness. But as a child, this was much harder to do.

I had a very unstable childhood and where I should have been transitioning through the stages of grief – although these stages aren't linear or simple – I was experiencing more traumatic events that added to the baggage I would eventually need to unpack.

I want to say that my story is unique. I want to believe that those who experience the loss of someone close to them can go through the various stages of grief without any added chaos or other unexpected circumstances. But this isn't true because life is unpredictable and it can take you by surprise, or shock. And most of the time, you learn to heal while also dealing with the extra chaos. You heal through the ups and downs. You heal through every sunrise and sunset. You heal through the adventures and the hard times, and every relationship and breakup. You just keep healing. You just keep healing.

But what does this look like when you're grieving?

Healing after loss is tough. It's not something that you can do in weeks, months or even years. Because although losing people is a guarantee in life, healing from that loss is not guaranteed. Even though we know that we will lose people, we hand them so much of ourselves that moving on from them after we lose them is one of the hardest things we must do.

Some days will feel harder than others. Some days will demand that you look at them directly, to find your deepest fears staring back at you. Some days will push you to the edge of your will and pull you back just before you decide to give up. And they will be hard, so, so hard. Days when the sun is still shining but you don't feel bright at all. Days when everyone around you is smiling but you can't bring yourself to feel the joy. Days when, no matter how much you tell yourself that you will be okay, you don't believe it. But it will be okay. Life is constantly fluctuating – the different shades of life are what allow you to grow, to change, to accept that life is not always going to be easy, but it is always worth living. Even through the difficult days, the hard-to-swallow days, the days when everything makes sense and nothing does at the same time – even those days. Life is always worth living.

How to Deal with Grief

Grief is an emotional response to loss, and as I've mentioned before, this loss is not limited to death. You go through grief when you lose a person, thing or even an experience. You can grieve the person you were meant to be. You can grieve the life you wanted to have. You can grieve broken relationships. You can grieve people even while they are alive. You can grieve those who never even lived, such as grieving a baby never born. There's no right or wrong way to grieve. Sometimes you feel numb, sometimes full of anger and hurt. Sometimes you're in denial that you experienced this loss and sometimes you're confused or even relieved (e.g., in cases where you had an estranged relationship).

When experiencing grief, you could go through the five stages of anger, denial, depression, bargaining and acceptance.

After you lose someone, it's possible that your emotions will become unpredictable, meaning you could be all over the place, and this feeling of being lost can be what affects you the most.

I remember doing a lot of bargaining as a child, especially when my dad would get sick. I made deals with God all the time. I uttered things in my mind like, 'I will do all my chores,' 'I will listen to Dad more' or 'I will go to sleep on time,' and in exchange, I asked Him to 'Make my dad stop drinking,' 'Give me a normal family' and 'Make everyone happy.' It was only when I was older that I understood I was grieving as a child. I was trying to move on from a loss I didn't completely understand, while worrying about another loss that I wasn't ready for.

How we see loss in this book is as follows: *when you lose someone, you lose a part of yourself.* Remember, ***just a part***. One way to think about this is to see the life that you share with others as a jigsaw puzzle. When you love someone, you hand them a piece of you, like a jigsaw piece that fits in perfectly with their life. In loving them, you hand that piece to them with the belief that they will always keep it, and they give you a piece of themselves which fits in perfectly with your life. But when you lose them, the jigsaw pieces that you handed each other are now missing, making your puzzle incomplete, making it feel like ***a part of you is missing***.

> *When you grieve someone that you've lost,
> what you're grieving is your own self – you're
> grieving the part of you that went with them.*

In moments like this, your main priority is to heal from this pain. Especially when you built so many memories and shared experiences with the person who's no longer here. Now, when you go to your local café, all you think about is the iced caramel latte and carrot cake that they loved; when you take your dog on a walk to the park, you remember their dog trotting along next to yours; when you crave your favourite dessert, you pine for the one that they'd make for you – and the piercing ache returns to the pit of your heart.

So, how do you heal from this and use self-love as a tool to guide you?

GRIEF LOOKS DIFFERENT FOR EVERYONE

Firstly, you accept that grief looks different for everyone. I've shared this in Chapter Two too (page 40). Often, we look at other people's healing journeys and compare them to our own, feeling uncomfortable that we haven't come through from this pain as quickly as them – but that's not a helpful way of looking at it. Everyone grieves in a unique way and their grieving period is different. For some people, grieving looks like getting back to work the next week and putting their head down. For others, it looks like spending weeks on end in bed and refusing to face the world. For some, grieving looks like booking a party holiday and drowning the pain with alcohol. For others, it looks like booking a self-care retreat and disappearing from the world for a few weeks.

None of these forms of grieving are 'incorrect', although some could be more harmful than others if you continue to do them indefinitely (such as seeking solace in alcohol, non-stop partying, running away from your responsibilities, etc.).

When you accept self-love into your healing journey, you learn to empathise with your pain a lot more. You treat your grieving period as you would a friend's. You let your heart grieve how it needs to, without comparing it to someone else's journey. And you understand that the grieving period differs from person to person, so instead of looking at what stage someone else is at, you look at what you need in the stage that *you are at* (acceptance, denial, anger, depression or bargaining).

Grief can look like:

* *Crying it out.*

* *Spending the day watching movies.*

✳   *Taking yourself on a walk.*

✳   *Expressing your feelings to a friend.*

✳   *Escaping to a different city for a few days.*

✳   *Not speaking to anyone for a while.*

✳   *Speaking to someone who knew them and sharing your memories.*

✳   *Engaging in self-care activities.*

✳   *Changing your environment.*

journal

Are you grieving the loss of someone/something? Remember, you can even grieve a life you wanted, a dream you had or the person you once were.

If yes, how did the loss make you feel and where are you in your journey currently? Is there a particular grieving stage you're at?

If you are not currently grieving, what are your views on grief?

Lastly, what similarities and differences can you see between different grief journeys, e.g., divorce, death, broken relationship, broken friendship, etc.?

When I look at my dad's grieving journey after my mum's death, it appears very different to mine. This doesn't mean that I've healed quicker than him, it just means that we grieved in different ways and have walked our own individual, unique healing journeys. But it took me a long time to accept this. I spent years blaming my dad for numbing his pain with alcohol or refusing to treat his depression. As though it was his fault that he wasn't able to heal in the way I'd seen others heal, or the way I had healed. I mean, sure, I was only four when my mum passed away, so my relationship with her was not as evolved as his was. She was his first and only love, after all. But still, I couldn't empathise with him, especially as a teenager, by which point I had spent most of my childhood pining for both of my parents.

It took a lot of effort and growth on my part to appreciate that we all grieve differently. Sometimes people spend years grieving but will reach a sense of normality in their lives, as was the case for me, but other times grief grows on you like second skin. You can't get rid of it. Instead, you create a new 'normal' for yourself, which could either make you better, or worse off. The latter was the case for my dad.

This is a huge part of grieving. If you lose someone close to you, your grieving experience, in comparison to your mum's, dad's or friend's, will be so unique that you can't look to those who are also grieving for the same person/thing/event for reference as to which stage you should be at. This also applies to your own grief journeys – no two journeys that you go on are the same.

I didn't understand this until I lost my uncle during the Covid-19 pandemic.

My uncle was like a father figure to me, having brought me up with my dad after my mum passed away and contributing to all my sweet, honeyed childhood memories. I felt his loss in my core and a part of me left with him and never returned. It was so difficult that my mind became a gloomy, relentless place, caging me for months after he passed. I smiled on the outside because I wanted to be strong for my family, but my chest always felt heavy. It would twist with every breath that I took. And that smile never reached my heart, it couldn't quell my pain, it couldn't make me feel warm.

I tried to get my mind off it by distracting myself. I went to see my friends. I spent more time with my partner, Ivnit. I focused on my work, and I made an effort to have a little bit of fun whenever I could. But occasionally when I felt happiness, laughing at my friend's joke or holding hands with Ivnit on a day out, my uncle's face would appear out of nowhere, suddenly making it hard to breathe. I could no longer function without darkness following me around. I couldn't write without hurting. I couldn't work out, read or go on walks and leave it all behind. I couldn't engage in any of the activities that I used to in the name of 'self-care' before he passed away.

Negative thoughts buzzed in my mind like loud bees, eating me inside out.

What was the point of it all?

What was the point in investing all my energy in trying to make my life 'right' when I couldn't control what would happen anyway?

When I couldn't stop the people that I loved from leaving me, what was the point in loving myself at all?

Because no matter what happened, the people I loved would leave and I would have to get used to living without them. The people I loved would take my heart with them and my chest would be empty all over again.

This loss felt a lot worse than the loss I felt when I was four.

The loss of my mum had truly changed my life, it had been the most impactful thing in my entire existence. But losing my uncle *hurt me more*. I could feel the pain pounding in my chest. Maybe because I knew him. I shared my life with him. I loved him and had been loved by him. Losing him felt so personal to me.

> whether it's big or small, bold or subtle — the feelings that arise after a traumatic event are often destructive, bleak and exhausting. But it's in these periods that you need light, hope and positivity the most. It's in these moments of being overwhelmed with hardship that you must adopt an attitude of love, care and empathy towards yourself.

I finally grasped the extent of my dad's grieving journey from my mum's death. Losing her must have felt so personal to him too. It must have felt as though he had lost a limb, because that's how I felt, and his pain was worse than mine, because she was his love, his life. It's a weird thing, healing from an untimely loss – one that you didn't see coming – because then you don't just grieve them, you grieve the life and experiences you've been robbed of, the life that you were supposed to live with them.

Deep down, we know that nothing will ever be the same after someone we love passes away, and that's what hurts us the most.

Think about what you currently need in this grieving journey. Write down as many ideas as you can. Refer to the points on pages 109 and 110 if you need guidance.

I want you to spend the next few weeks doing at least one of these things, e.g., cry it out, talk to someone, escape to a different city, change your environment, engage in self-care, etc.

NOTHING STAYS THE SAME

Practising self-love in my healing brought to light a lot of things, one of which was being able to act on the following thought: **nothing stays the same**.

To begin with, we are never the same. We grow. We change. Sometimes we're kind and sometimes we say cruel things that are a shock even to our own ears. Especially when we're healing and hurting. Especially when we're grieving and failing to move on. Those moments make us very bitter. Those moments can bring out the worst in us.

But when you walk on the path to self-love, you acknowledge this about yourself. You don't like it. You don't even appreciate it – that you have the power to be spiteful and mean – but you still accept it. Because it's who you are. Both the best parts of you and the worst.

In the same way, relationships change too. They evolve. They become something else. Sometimes we lose those people entirely, through death, distance or circumstances. And although the expectation that our relationships will last forever is what gives those relationships meaning, this expectation also stops us from welcoming joy once more in our lives or developing the strength to move on when those relationships end. It's for this reason that when they end – because *nothing lasts forever* – we're unable to cope. We're unable to let go and move forward, because this person leaving affected the normal trajectory of our lives to such an extent that we don't know how to make sense of our lives now.

When you're grieving from the loss of a loved one, what will help you heal is embracing that *change is inevitable*. People are bound to leave your life. Whether through death, whether through relationships falling apart or whether through the constant flux of life – not everyone will stay with you forever.

> Just as the seasons rise and fall, the sun sets
> for the night to soar, people also come and go.
> In fact, the only constant of life is that
> nothing stays the same. Especially people.

The one thing that will change your life forever is accepting that everything is temporary. Happiness. Pain. Failure. Success. Your relationships. Your entire existence is temporary and the fact that you can't be sure whether you will live another day is enough to show you that whatever it is you're stressing about, it will pass. Happiness and pain are both fleeting, sprinkled throughout the larger chapters that make up our entire lives. Lives that can pass with a blink of an eye. So, what's the point of comparison? Of wanting what other people have and feeling like a failure if you don't get it? What is the point of holding grudges and letting your ego direct your behaviour, and letting your mind take hold of your relationships in a way that your heart wouldn't? Knowing that this exact moment will never come back should be enough to urge you to pick up the phone and make that call. It should be enough to make you realise that if you're in a difficult place right now — hurting, frustrated, upset over something that you don't have any control over — give yourself time. You won't be here forever. Neither in pain, nor in happiness. So, make the most of it. Forgive more easily, learn to push away the bad stuff and accept growth in ways that benefit not just you but everyone around you. Let go of all the negative feelings and animosity and be kind. Be soft. Be gentle with other people. And remind yourself that if today was painful, if today was awful, if today was nothing like what you had hoped it would be — tomorrow will be better. Tomorrow will be better.

REPLACE REGRET WITH COMPASSION

With the false belief that our relationships will last (although sub-consciously we know that they won't), we start to make a common mistake: we take our relationships for granted. We stop checking up on our loved ones. We don't call and text often. We don't even meet them for months at a time. We assume that they must be okay, and as they continue their normal routine in the background, it allows us to continue our normal routine in the foreground. Until something shocking happens – they die, or they leave – and we learn how mis-taken we were.

When my uncle passed away, I felt a lot of regret. Regret over not checking up on him more often. Regret that there was so much that I no longer had the opportunity to say. This made me feel worse about myself. How could I not find a minute in my day to call him, to ask him if he needed anything? How could I not see him in over a year? This made me feel guilty and angry at myself, and my grieving him correlated with my self-loathing. Somehow it became less about losing a father-figure and more about my failures as a *daughter* to him, and how I should have, could have, would have done more – but now all these things were 'what ifs' and I was to blame.

This isn't a healthy way of grieving someone, and maybe you haven't engaged in this form of self-talk, if you're a smart cookie. But if you have felt/are feeling regret or self-loathing in your griev-ing journey, this is how I want you to tackle it.

I want you to change the story that you tell yourself.

Losing someone isn't a failure on your part. In a way, it represents a success: you got to share a portion of your life with them, you got to give them a piece of you and take a piece of them. Losing some-one doesn't mean you have lost out on something. It means you've gained so much from the time that you got to share with them.

Losing someone doesn't mean that everything is over. It means that this chapter has closed, but the experiences you had with them are laced into your story and you will take these memories forward with you forever.

During grief, you can be your own biggest enemy. Even if you checked up on the person you lost every week or month, you may still feel like you didn't do enough. You may still feel like you didn't go all the way. And maybe you did. Maybe your mind is so clouded with the pain of losing this person that you can't see beyond it. Maybe you were there through all the highs and lows, but you can't see it right now because you're stuck. And maybe you didn't. Maybe you forgot and were tired after work. Maybe you kept telling yourself that you would call them but you never did and then it was too late.

But don't beat yourself up about it.

Because life isn't black and white, and neither are the mistakes that we make. We go through different things from day to day but it all washes away when one single thought overwhelms us, and that thought could be as simple as: 'You didn't call them enough.' You forget everything. You forget that there was a big project at work. You forget that your mum was sick, and you were busy with her. You forget that you had recently experienced a heartbreak and were healing. You forget that you were tired and fed up and just didn't want to see anyone for a while. You forget that you had your own mental health problems and needed someone yourself.

And you self-loathe. You think about everything you should have done while this person was in your life, but you forget just how much you went through in that period too.

Empathise with yourself. Develop compassion.

Losing people is not the end of your happiness. And you can't let it become the end of the love that you hold for yourself either. Instead of telling yourself, 'I've lost this incredible person, and I will never be the same,' tell yourself, 'I am so lucky to have been affected by this person. I am so lucky that I shared this much time with them. I'm grateful for the influence and hold they had over my life, and I will take all the memories, all the lessons and all the love forward with me.'

It can feel like you've lost yourself, but if you think about it, the years of loving them and being loved by them gave you back so much more than you gave away. It gave you so much more than you gave away.

> *Self-love changes everything for you because you no longer compare your grieving journey to others', you no longer rush it and you're no longer hard on yourself or others because of it.*

Nothing Will Ever Be the Same, and That's Okay

Embracing self-love in your grieving journey helps you in so many ways, because you're no longer afraid of going through the various stages of grief.

If you need to sob, and break down on the floor of your apartment, you do it. If you need to hide under the covers for the entire weekend and binge watch Netflix because real people are too much effort, you do it. But you also hug yourself. You hold your own hand. You push your body off the ground. You stop telling yourself 'I will never be okay again' and instead, you remind yourself how strong you are. You take a tub of ice cream and finish the whole thing, because that's what you need.

You watch the worst TV shows and the best. You watch *their favourite shows* because you miss them. You listen to their voice messages; you look over past photos and videos and you let yourself grieve. You remind yourself of the good times and you forget the bad.

Self-love changes you. You no longer say,
'Nothing will be the same again' with a sour
aftertaste, and instead, you say it with hope:
'Nothing will be the same again, but I'm ready
for what's to come in the future.'

You stop telling yourself that you've lost yourself in the process. Yes, you've lost a part of who you were. You've lost a side of your life that you might never get back. But this is why you keep being there for yourself. It's a reason to keep loving yourself. Because even though it's hard right now, and it will be tomorrow, the positive actions that you take today will affect how you heal from this. And to heal from this, you need to hold on to all the good, and let go of the bad, as much as you can.

This doesn't mean that you immediately start preparing for the marathon that you were training for before you experienced this loss, or finish writing that business proposal, or plan the grand wedding that you're not feeling anymore. It doesn't mean that you force yourself to do what no longer feels right.

Instead, it means that you hold your own hand and take one step at a time.

If you feel low, let yourself feel low. But on the days that you're feeling good, don't condemn yourself for being *happy* so quickly after this loss, don't let guilt overpower you on the days you're doing well. Doing well doesn't mean that you've forgotten them, or that you didn't value them enough. Doing well doesn't mean that losing them didn't affect you. Doing well doesn't detract from their value. Doing well means that you're accepting the loss and learning to live with it and move on. Doing well means that you're learning to be happy again.

Let yourself do better. Let yourself get up in the morning. Let yourself smile, and laugh, and carry out the tiny actions of self-love that you used to before. Don't beat yourself up for feeling a little bit of joy within a few days, weeks or months of grieving, because you deserve to be happy.

Losing someone else doesn't mean that you have lost yourself too.

It is during the healing journeys that result from traumatic events, that embracing self-love can create waves of growth in your life, becoming the catalyst for your happiness going forward.

Life is like a constantly flowing river, always moving, always changing. There are flashes of happiness and bursts of pain, and 'nothing lasts forever' is at the tip of our tongue every time it all falls apart. But it is true — nothing lasts forever. Happiness is fleeting, pain temporary and love, love changes with every season. And I know that this world makes it seem like something is wrong with you if you're feeling low, I know that this world makes it hard to be heartbroken, lost or hurting, but there's nothing wrong with your life if you're going through a difficult time. Accept each emotion and let yourself experience it entirely — joy, discomfort, love, excitement, nostalgia, all of it. Because the tide will turn and what you experience today will disappear tomorrow, which means that living in the moment is all that you truly have. And sometimes life feels like the biggest blessing you could receive, sometimes it feels like you're on top of the world and nothing could be better than this. And other times, it is hard, it is so incredibly hard. But that is okay. Because everything is temporary, every emotion fleeting and all you really have in this ever-expanding universe is this present moment. All you really have is today.

chapter 5

relationships and self-love

I can't begin to express how important relationships are in your healing journey and, specifically, your path to self-love.

The early attachments that you form help shape your self-perception; they are the primary constructs for your moral values, and they direct the quality of relationships that you will later build. Relationships also affect your present life – as through them you can either enjoy a nourished, happy existence or tolerate an unhealthy, uncomfortable one.

On your path to self-love, pay close attention to the people that you surround yourself with, as that will determine how well – successful, effective, impactful, life-changing, you get the gist – your healing journey from that heartbreak, failure, loss, etc. goes.

As part of your self-love path, you need to unlearn all the toxic relationship patterns that you have in your life. One way in which to do this is to turn to, and unpack, the early relationships that you formed – i.e., with your family – and another way to do this is to *look at your current relationships* and carefully analyse those patterns with the aim of bettering them.

The relationships you form shape your
personality, your worldview, your values and
the choices that you make. <u>we're social beings,
after all</u>. So, when you get the choice, choose
the life where you're surrounded by
compassionate and kind individuals rather
than selfish ones.

But how do you change the relationship dynamics in your life?
There's a lot that you can do, and this *includes* the relationships
that you formed in the footings of your childhood. In this chapter,
you will learn that you can either remove toxic, chaotic people from
your life or find new ways to meet those that you love halfway.

journal

*What does your ideal physical safe space look like? E.g., a
tranquil room with plants, a library, a cottage by the beach,
an outdoor sunset with a lit fire, home.*

*What kind of people would you like to see in this space?
Write any names of those close to you that also come
to mind.*

What I would tell my ten-year-old-self: don't be afraid to make new friends and show them how funny, kind and goofy you are. Give your parents a kiss before you leave for school and a hug before you go to bed, don't cringe and utter the words, 'You're embarrassing me in front of my friends' when they pull your cheek, or tuck your shirt in. These precious interactions will never come back. Embrace it. Make the most of this childlike joy, the fact that you can swing as high as you want in the park, and run, jump and scream at the top of your lungs without having to worry about what others will think. Have birthday parties, as many as you can. Put that silly, colourful hat on and dance to crazy music, and don't worry. Don't worry about the argument that you overheard between your parents, or that conversation about the bills, or about what grades you will get in school, and whether you will make everyone proud. Don't burden yourself with problems you don't yet have and instead enjoy this youth, this moment in your life that you will never get back. Let yourself be fluent in happiness and sunshine. Don't let the rigidness of life snatch your innocence away. Dance, laugh and be the child that you're supposed to be. It is not your time to grow up yet. It is not your time.

Enjoy a Safe Support Circle

Maybe you have started to move on from a painful event and you're still not where you want to be. Perhaps you're practising both easy and tough self-love to take better care of yourself, but still not getting the results. Still not feeling better about the original experience that set off this process. Still not *feeling okay*, at least not for long enough. You might have a few theories as to why you don't feel okay, or maybe you still haven't been able to figure out why.

Why does journalling not relieve the weight off your chest? Why is it that when you meet up with a friend, you feel even more drained afterwards? Why don't all those self-care days, meditation retreats and yoga exercises help? Why is it that even after you go to therapy, you feel stuck in the same place when you return home? Why is it that no matter what you try to do to love yourself, you find yourself straying further and further away from healing your heart?

The answer is because even though you're doing the work to help yourself, those around you aren't. The people that you surround yourself with. The environment that you've built at work. Your social circle. The place that you call home. Those individuals that you let into your safe space, into your support circle – to help you, to guide you along the way – *they are still wrong for you*.

Even though you're doing the work that's required of you, you're not changing your space. You're not shifting your environment. You're not removing those who are damaging your peace. They are still there. They still have a hold over you. The people who treat you badly. The people who bring negative energy into your life. The people who take more than they give. The people who – in fact – are not right for you, but are all you've ever known.

Until you cut them out of your life, or at least draw necessary boundaries to protect yourself, you can't walk on the path to self-love or reap its benefits and move forward.

LET'S BUILD A SAFE SPACE

A nurturing support circle with your loved ones can help you to:

✳ *Boost your self-worth.*

✳ *Increase your joy and happiness.*

✳ *Provide you with a safe space.*

✳ *Decrease negative emotions.*

✳ *Encourage you to take new adventures.*

✳ *Push you out of your comfort zone.*

✳ *Give you a sense of belonging.*

✳ *Decrease loneliness.*

Having a safe support circle with people who help you rather than create hurdles for you is so important for self-love to be effective in your life. For example, if you feel safe with your family/friends who are super considerate, then you know that you can say anything to them and feel listened to. But if you don't feel safe with them then you will be more fearful about expressing yourself, because telling them what you're going through may result in backlash, making you feel worse about your situation.

When you practise self-love, it's important that you surround yourself with people who affirm those encouraging, uplifting thoughts that you're developing. To make the most of your path to self-love, you need a support circle of people who raise you up, respect and love you, want the best for you and do their bit to remind you that you're worth all the love that you've started giving yourself.

> *During your self-love journey, the quality of your relationships guide action and inaction on your part. They can either motivate you to put yourself first or pull you towards self-neglect.*

Imagine that you're carrying out one or more of the following actions with the intent to practise self-love: going for daily walks, taking a trip, visiting a counsellor, reading books, watching TV, having difficult conversations, meeting up with your mum for brunch, keeping to yourself for the weekend, etc. Now imagine that you receive criticism from your loved ones for these activities – for telling them that you are visiting a counsellor, for taking up healthier eating habits so you couldn't go for late night ice cream with them for fear of temptation or for cancelling dinner because you wanted to keep to yourself and couldn't bear to leave the house.

If you receive constant backlash when you practise self-love – the kind that's unjustified and, deep down, comes from disregard for you – then this is a sign for you to re-evaluate your relationships. Ask yourself: are these people good for your health and welfare? Because in cases such as this, your loved ones are blaming you for prioritising yourself instead of thinking about what their part is in supporting you on your path to self-love.

The people you include in your support circle have a responsibility towards you – such as checking up on you when you don't leave the house, or supporting you in your healthy eating habits by encouraging you to further work on yourself.

And in cases where you practise self-love but aren't comfortable in sharing it with them, you need to ask yourself why this is the case.

Why can't you tell them how you're feeling?

Have they done something in the past that stopped you from being honest?

> when you're surrounded by people who
> appreciate, value and respect you, it's easier
> to accept the love you give to yourself. It's
> very hard to say no to self-love — instead, you
> naturally find yourself walking on that path
> and healing along the way.

exercise

Pay attention to the patterns present in your current relationships and ask yourself a few questions:

✳ *Is the balance tipping in favour of unhappiness instead of joy in my relationship?*

✳ *Am I constantly putting them first and myself last?*

✳ *Has my life changed for the better after forming this relationship?*

✳ *Do I enjoy spending time with this person, or would I rather stay away?*

✳ *Do I feel uneasy when I see my phone ring with their name*
   popping up on the front screen?

Answering these questions will allow you to figure out whether
*or not someone is **'good'** for you (healthy for your heart, mind*
and soul).

It will also highlight a lot of crucial feelings that you may have
buried inside a compartment of your mind regarding your
current relationships. These are the kinds of feelings that are
important for you to deal with if you want to progress in your
healing journey and practise self-love.

How I practise self-love: each morning I tell myself, 'Today is a new day,' giving myself a chance to do it all over again. This helps set the mood for the day. Even if things hadn't gone well the night before, I don't carry that feeling forward with me. I express my emotions — to myself, to my friends, to my family. I tell people what's bothering me when it bothers me. I don't keep it in. I try to let go — of people, of situations, of emotions. And when I can't let go, then I spend time with myself to understand why I'm feeling this way. I love people, but I also love spending time alone — so, I find a delicate balance. I don't go to bed upset because I know that I won't get a good night's sleep if I do. I try to be mindful of my triggers and remove myself from situations that could be harmful for me. If I want to go somewhere, I make the plans. I don't wait for others to take me out, instead I take them out and make them feel special too. I don't hold grudges for lost friendships. If we've distanced, then it's because we're both busy with our lives — it isn't just one person's fault. This helps unburden me from negative emotions, and I feel lighter. I treat myself to chocolate chip cookies, shopping, adventures and good books, just because. I repeat the phrase 'My happiness is my responsibility' every single day.

Remove Toxic People

One crisp October morning in 2014, 19-year-old me bumped into a girl who I'll call Radhi. I was already following her on social media because of our mutuals but I had not yet met her in person. So, when I saw her silhouette in front of me, I called out her name – an action that I regret to this day. We introduced ourselves and spoke animatedly, and I was chuffed that I had finally made a new friend. I was in my second year at university and after having lots of close friends at school, I was feeling extremely lonely. For this reason, meeting someone new excited me – I was looking forward to what this interaction would entail.

After speaking for a few minutes, we hugged and set a lunch date for the following week, leaving with a candied goodbye on our lips. What I didn't expect was for that lunch to go as horribly as it did. But there I was, a week later, in agonising pain during the hour that I spent with her. And when we *finally* said goodbye, I made a mental note and metaphorically stuck it on my forehead to remind myself to stay away from her.

Radhi wasn't horrible. She didn't say anything offensive, shout or treat me badly during our lunch. Nor did I think I was too good to be her friend. But during the hour that I spent with Radhi, I found myself rejecting her energy. We had such different views about life and what we wanted, her opinions about the world felt alien to me and I couldn't find myself connecting with her on any level – and alignment in these are the basic foundation of long-lasting friendships. And perhaps this was a huge red sign for me to not get into a friendship with her; it was my inner voice telling me that we weren't going to be a good fit going forward.

Have you ever spent time with someone and internally recoiled? Does hearing them talk make you wince, because you don't accept anything that comes out of their mouth, either because it's offensive, ridiculous to your eyes or conflicts with your morals? Have you ever met someone who, even after several meetups, hasn't been able to make that connection with your heart? You can't imagine letting them in, being their friend or being inspired by them? If you have, then I highly recommend that you remove that person from your life right now if you haven't already. I mean it.

Energy is a huge thing. If you don't enjoy someone's presence, then let me assure you that *it will only get worse*.

Did I follow my own advice? *Not really, no.*

Is it because I'm an idiot? *Kind of*, but hear me out.

> When you walk on the path to self-love, one of the first steps to take is removing the pattern of toxic relationships in your life.

There were a few reasons why I couldn't cut off the friendship with Radhi before it developed, but mainly I was 19 and had not mastered the art of saying 'no'. And although I, at least at first, didn't initiate any more plans with her myself, we were drawn together repeatedly by our mutual friends.

In the time that I knew Radhi, we did become good friends. We met up often and would catch up on the phone, and I grew close to her over the years. I became her go-to person when she was upset, and she became someone that I relied on whenever I had a crisis. In my defence, I barely had any friends – both in and out of university – at the time we got to know each other, at least not those that I could say were '*my people*'. My high school friends and I had all parted ways, and I had not found anyone since then that I could develop a strong bond with, so Radhi's friendship gave me that flicker of hope that I wasn't alone. That felt good.

But I should have known that although she was someone I

became heavily reliant on, she wasn't *my person* either – my first date with her confirmed this. It wasn't until years later that I did the self-reflection as part of my path to self-love and I understood her friendship had been toxic all along.

Radhi was toxic for me because in the time that I knew her, my self-worth had plummeted unbelievably, even more than before.

A normal conversation with Radhi consisted of her criticising my appearance, my decisions and my personality. She made me feel clueless about my life and reminded me that I needed her because I was prone to making bad choices. She also never failed to point out when my arse looked flat, when my skin was all over the place or how childish my hairstyle appeared. But she didn't say any of those words maliciously. She would laugh it off in conversation. She didn't sneer at me or look down on me. In fact, she would look sincere, mirroring the same concerned expression of the family member who had first called me fat. And because of this, for years I thought that her actions were normal. As though she was doing me a service by '*constructively*' criticising me, as though her words were essential to my self-improvement, and I should note down everything that she uttered.

I didn't particularly appreciate the gossiping either. The consistent back-talking about others, the negativity, the two-facedness towards our friends and peers: it all gave me the ick. Initially, I waved it all off. I reminded myself that not everyone was perfect, and deep down she had a good heart, no matter how many bad things she had to say about others. And wasn't she always there for me? Wasn't she always reaching out to see if I was okay? *She's a good friend*, I kept saying. *She's a good friend*.

What affected me most was her continually comparing me to my cousin, who was also in our group. This triggered me. You will remember me mentioning in Chapter Three (page 67) that I spent much of my childhood being matched against my cousin. This constant comparison gave me years of trauma that had already damaged my self-worth by the time I met Radhi.

Deep down, I didn't believe that I was worthy, and Radhi's behaviour deepened this belief.

> Toxic people are like a disease to your self-love journey. They attack all the good in your life and make you doubt yourself. They don't leave room for growth, for self-discovery. They only push for self-neglect, for self-denial. They make you question your worth. So, question why you have them in your life to begin with.

You might not think that Radhi's behaviour was *deep*, or hurtful. Many of you have had friends who were worse. I promise you that I've had some crazy, toxic friends in my life too, and I've been a victim of lot of gaslighting and ill-treatment. Those friends have long vanished into my past. But for some reason – perhaps because of my childhood trauma of being bullied about my weight, hair and skin colour – Radhi's friendship was really damaging, and after her, I've refused to accept people like that in my life.

And if I had known all along that her behaviour was toxic for me, I would have run ages ago.

You get to choose who you want to be. You get to choose who you allow into the creases of your heart. You get to choose the hands that make you come undone and the arms that hold you. You get to choose the people that you let into your life, and the love that you want. And I hope you choose yourself as well. I hope you see all the good that is in your life and stop focusing on the bad. I hope you change the story that you tell yourself about your past and see yourself as the main character instead — as the person who, despite the odds, changed their life for the better. I hope you realise how far you've come from where you were. Because life isn't easy most of the time — things are bound to go wrong. But I hope you to let go of the pain and choose happiness instead.

journal

Do you have someone in your life who you would label as 'toxic'?

Who are they to you? E.g., friend, colleague, parent, cousin, etc.

Have you done anything to change this dynamic?

Do you think this relationship can be saved?

If you had a chance to, would you remove them from your life?

I would have booked a first-class ticket out of our friendship and indulged in a gooey self-love chocolate cake on the way, washing it down with milky, positive affirmations that would drain all the criticism that came from her out of my system. I would have sent her a postcard from my new condo, in the city of positive energies, delivering the final message – that I no longer wanted to be her friend.

When I was working on myself as part of my path to self-love, it occurred to me that the reason I didn't do this initially is because of my childhood trauma. Because of the emotional abuse I experienced, I craved friendships with girls like Radhi. I searched for validation and strived to do better when I received constant criticism because that's what I was used to – searching for that rare compliment that made all the belittlement worth it. Through my childhood and adolescence I'd been made to feel less and been teased for my appearance. Radhi was a reflection of what I'd always known.

The realisation hit me unexpectedly, or maybe it had been building up for years and finally came to the fore, when I started my toughest healing journey at 21.

Suddenly, a lightbulb lit, and I saw all the darkness of our friendship that I had hidden behind the dusty cloud of excuses that I'd made for her over the years.

Sure, I would go to Radhi when I had a problem, but how many times had she actually supported me? Instead, she was belittling me. She made me feel small. She would wave off solutions that I offered to my problems and supply solutions of her own, solutions that I always agreed were better than mine but – now that I reflected – had done me more harm than good. I thought back to all the good times that we shared and then finally focused on the bad. The ugly truth. The fact that I had been justifying her harmful actions, burying the parts of her that I didn't like behind the ones that I did, when, sadly, she had been reinstating the same behaviours that had damaged my self-worth and self-esteem for so long. She had been harming me emotionally. She was toxic for me.

After our fallout, which didn't involve a confrontation as much as it did a concluding argument over the phone, I ran and didn't look back. I deleted her number. I unfollowed her on social media. I wiped my phone clean of her photos, messages and memories – much like the process of a romantic breakup. Because this was a breakup indeed – it was a friendship breakup, one that I should've executed years ago. A part of me still regrets that I never got my closure with her, that I never got to tell her how she had made me feel during those years. But that doesn't matter, because I finally, *finally*, decided to put my foot down and drag out the unwelcome guest from my safe space.

Remember, toxic people can be found in all kinds of relationships, not just friendships. For instance, your relationship with your family tremendously affects the quality of your life. Being in a nourishing, safe family where you're encouraged to take care of yourself will result in higher levels of self-esteem as an adult, resulting in your continuing to engage in healthy, heartening relationships that further your growth. But if you're surrounded by people who insult you and treat you with disregard then you're less likely to treat yourself with compassion as an adult, and instead you will pursue relationships where you constantly seek validation and love.

> There isn't much that you can do when it comes to changing the foundations of your childhood – those experiences have passed, the damage has been done and the trauma that you carry forward with you is a challenge that you now need to face. But you can change how you <u>think</u>, <u>react</u>, <u>behave</u> and <u>feel</u> about your past, as well as move on from those who have hurt you.

Similarly, toxic people can be found in dating/romantic relationships/situationships. And often these are the ones that can really affect your self-esteem as an adult.

Having been in a few *'situationships'* myself, I can conclude that people who give you mixed signals, have one foot in and one foot out, and speak in riddles rather than tell you where you belong in their life are wasting your time. They're keeping you hooked just long enough for them to find someone else. Their heart just isn't in it.

Not having your heart in a relationship with someone that

you're getting to know is fine – but clear and honest communica-
tion in any relationship, even one in its early stages, is necessary.
Stringing someone along isn't fine. Making them believe that they
mean something to you just so you can hold on to them until you
find someone better isn't fine. Making promises that you can't keep
isn't fine. Not loving someone but holding on to them for your own
selfish reasons isn't fine – because you're stopping them from find-
ing someone who *will* love them in the way that they deserve. You're
stopping them from finding someone who *will* fit into their life the
way a partner is supposed to. You're stopping them from finding
happiness, and that isn't okay.

The people who engage in the kinds of relationships that I've
outlined above are toxic for your well-being. Whether you're dating
them, or whether they are a member of your family, they are toxic
for you because they leech off the negative self-narratives you
create in your mind because of them. They gain power from your
weaknesses.

So, regain your power by walking on the path to self-love and
removing any and all toxic people from your life.

journal

*Thinking back to the toxic person you identified earlier, if
you were to sit them down, what would you say to them
about how they treat you?*

*Do you think they would change? If not, then you know
what to do.*

Over the years, I've learned a lot about people. I understand now that some people just won't change. No matter how much you wish that they will. No matter how many excuses you make to keep them in your life — they just won't change. The cycle that you find yourself in, the one of them hurting you, then justifying it (or not), then you forgiving them and moving on until they hurt you again, will go on forever until you put a stop to it. If someone's presence in your life is harmful, if it's damaging to your mental and emotional health, if they're no longer nourishing your growth and positively contributing to your life — then let them go. If, even after setting boundaries, telling them what bothers you and laying down your expectations, they haven't changed, then believe me when I tell you: <u>they will never change</u>. You may not be able to control how other people treat you, but you can control who you let into your safe circle, and into your heart. Make wise choices. Protect yourself.

FIND NEW PEOPLE. FIND A NEW YOU.

My self-esteem didn't start soaring after Radhi was out, because there was still a lot of tough self-love work that I needed to take part in. The healing work that forces you to ask yourself questions, to put yourself in an uncomfortable position so you can figure out why you keep getting into these relationships, why you're attracted to those kinds of people, why you let others treat you poorly; answers which can be found in the depths of your foundational years.

For the next few years, this is the truth I followed.

As a result, I let new people into my safe space – people who were careful with my heart. People who cheered me up when I was low and made me laugh when I was in tears. People who didn't make me question myself. People who were there for me, who provided me with an environment where I felt listened to, where I felt understood. Their words, encouragement and love helped me as I was finding myself. I recovered faster. I felt joyful. More fulfilled. I enjoyed my own presence. My smiles filled my face and even tingled my insides – which was something that hadn't happened for years before.

I also uncovered why I had struggled so much until then. Why I couldn't get over my childhood trauma, why I held on to one-sided love, why I let people continue to treat me a certain way: *because struggling was all I'd ever known*. I wasn't familiar with the other side of love – the side where you witness empathy from those who will always be there for you.

The side that is filled with delicate souls who will try their best to never let you down.

Once I wiped my slate clean of toxic friendships and unhealthy attachments, there was so much room for healthy relationships. For good hearts. For compassion. There was so much more room for self-love.

Before I realised it, I was growing, uncovering hidden parts of myself, and discovering layers of a new me – one that I really liked. I was becoming someone else, as well as learning who I was at the same time, and *it was magical*.

I was beginning to like this person that I was becoming. I was beginning to love me.

What are your favourite things about the people closest to you?

If there was one beautiful trait that you could take from them, what would it be?

Now, it's time that you turn to your relationships and write down a list of everyone that is close to you.

After this, ask yourself, 'Is each person adding something valuable to my life?' This question has been split into smaller questions below, which I want you to answer in as much detail as possible, not just with 'yes' or 'no'.

✳   *Do they positively influence your self-worth?*

✳   *Do they increase your happiness?*

✳   *Do they provide you with a safe space?*

✳   *Does spending time with them make you feel negative/ positive emotions?*

✳   *Do they encourage you to take on new adventures?*

✳   *Do they push you out of your comfort zone?*

✳   *Does having them in your life give you a sense of belonging?*

✳   *Does being around them decrease your loneliness?*

When walking on the path to self-love, it's essential that you remove toxic people from your support circle. To do this, you need to reflect. Try to remember your last few interactions with the people close to you. Think about how you felt when you saw them. Recall whether they made you smile and laugh, or if something they said made you feel good about yourself. Count the number of times they've been there for you, picture in your mind all your celebrations that they've been a part of.

Would you call them if you were feeling lonely and needed someone to talk to, or as an escape from your destructive thoughts?

Through this exercise, you will identify the people who help you flourish and those who thwart your potential. Maybe the results are a surprise. You might find that those you barely meet up with

light up your life, and you will want to increase how much time
you spend with them. You may find that those you give most of
your energy to are the joy-sucking vampires that you should stay
away from – in which case you will want to limit how much of
yourself you give to them.

Remember, you could have a healthy relationship with someone
and still battle with conflicting emotions regarding parts of their
personality – for instance, having a great friend who never lets you
down but has stayed in contact with your abusive ex. Just like this,
there will be various shades of grey to consider when you look fur-
ther into your relationships.

When exercising self-love not only are you deciding which rela-
tionships to stick with, which to work on and which to let go of,
you're also learning about your own role in the growth and break-
down of those relationships. Relationships are not one way, and
self-love means showing up for others as well as showing up for your-
self. For this reason, self-love will demand from you *that you learn to
do better too.* And if you haven't learned how, don't worry, because
by the end of this book, you will be so capable of balancing self-love
with your love for others.

The one truth that we need to accept about life is that even when you find 'your people', those people are not going to stay with you forever. Because sometimes you find those once-in-a-lifetime people — you know, the ones with rough edges, messy souls and the biggest heart you've ever seen. People who take your hand and hold it as tight as they can to remind you that they won't let go. People who make you feel comfortable in being vulnerable. People who mean it when they say that they're here for you. Because sometimes you can find those once-in-a-lifetime people — the ones who make you laugh when you're in tears, and dance under the rain, the ones who fill your bucket with so much happiness that you don't know what to do with it — and yet they still leave. You still lose them. You still grow apart. You still fall apart. You still end up walking on your path alone. Until you find new people. New once-in-a-lifetime individuals who will change you, love you, tire your bones out with new adventures and give you forever memories to take forward. Because that's just how it is. Because life is constantly evolving, and people are never forever. Because even though we wish it didn't — 'your people' often means 'your people at that moment in your life' and nothing more. Nothing more.

SELF-LOVE AND RELATIONSHIPS ARE
INTIMATELY ATTACHED

Some of you will struggle with the idea of having bitter conversations about toxic behaviour or removing people from your life, and I can understand that it's hard. It's hard to tell yourself to cut out a family member or take some space away from them because you love them. It's hard to admit that a friendship of ten years has done you more harm than good, because you remember all the good times. Because then it seems like over a decade of your life was wasted. It seems like you're letting your family down. It seems like you're going to isolate yourself from all those who care about you.

It seems, it seems, it seems. But it isn't what matters.

What matters is you enjoying stable mental and emotional health. What matters is you having nurturing beliefs about who you are. What matters is prioritising people *who will prioritise you*. People who mean it when they say that they love you, because you see it in their actions. People who don't need to tell you that they're here for you – as that's where you will always find them.

> Self-love and relationships are intimately attached, so make sure that the important relationships in your life are nourishing you, especially when you're learning to love yourself.

The basic philosophy to take forward in your path to self-love is that healthy relationships bring you happiness, and toxic relationships cause you pain. So, it's clear what to do, right? Aim to have healthy relationships with good individuals. Only then can you manifest self-love into your life. Only then can you continue to heal.

In your path to self-love, what matters to you most about your relationships?

How have other people helped you on your self-love journey?

Self-Love Leaves Room for Love

You're currently on the path to self-love. You're learning more about your trauma. You're moving on from the past and embracing a new you. *But you can't do this while you're in a relationship. You can't do this if you get into a relationship. You can't do this with someone else by your side. That's what you tell yourself.* **Or. Or. Or.** *You can't do this* **until you get into a relationship** *because you need someone loving you to know that you're worthy of love.*

A lot of people foster these thoughts, but these thoughts are false. The truth is, you can take the self-love journey whether you want to find love, you're in love or you're happily single.

Let me clarify that if you want to find love, don't do it with the belief that finding a relationship will heal or complete you. The answers that you're looking for can't be found in other people. Your healing isn't dependent on a romantic partner.

Of course, it's okay to both be open to relationships and be on the path to self-love, because those are two different walkways in your life, and they work really well together.

You don't need a partner to heal you or mend your broken heart. You don't need a partner to learn how to love yourself. You don't need a partner to know who you truly are. You can do all those things by yourself. But your partner can support you. They can remind you that they love you when you seem to forget. They can hold your hand, stand beside you and be your biggest cheerleader as you face some of the toughest hurdles. They can be that light that guides you, reminding you that they will be here while you heal. They will be here while you heal.

What is your relationship status? How does this make you feel?

If you're single, are you open to finding love? If so, what are your reasons for looking for love?

If you're in a relationship, how does your partner support you in practising self-love?

If you're happy and single, what are the best parts?

If you're happy and in a relationship, what are the best parts?

TRUE SOUL-SEARCHING DOESN'T DEPEND ON YOUR RELATIONSHIP STATUS

There's emerged a cultural hype, perpetuated by social media, which puts the spotlight on this idea that *true soul-searching happens alone*. You've probably seen TikToks of people going on adventures by themselves, booking a cabin in the woods, reading, doing yoga, smiling at the camera with a motivational voiceover which singles out words such as 'alone' and 'comfortable' and 'complete'.

It's great that we have a culture where being **single** and **enough** is valued. Especially for women, because it wasn't until relatively recently that we were no longer viewed by society as **less** when we didn't have a male companion.

But I'm worried about how this widespread ideology looks for those who are finding themselves and looking for love at the same time, or those who are struggling with self-love and are currently in a relationship. Because it implies that they should stop looking for love, or get out of that relationship, if they are to *truly work on* themselves.

But this isn't usually the best route going forward.

This culture of 'single life is the best life' promotes a way of thinking, especially among the younger generation, that declares: *'Until I love me, I can't love you.'* This means that until you reach this point where you know yourself completely and love that version of you – which is impossible, because soul-searching continues throughout your life – you shouldn't look for love or be in a relationship.

I'm not saying that single life isn't the best life, and I'm not saying that it is – instead, the best life is the one that *brings you happiness*, and this isn't dependent on your relationship status. You can be in a relationship and be unhappy or be in a healthy relationship which makes you the happiest person alive (I'm living proof of this). You could be single and very lonely, or you could be alone and having the adventure of a lifetime, surrounded by your loved ones, taking each day as it comes.

The path to self-love doesn't tell you whether to find love or not find love. The path to self-love leaves it open for you to decide whether being in a relationship will benefit you or not. But it does acknowledge how important relationships in general are, and if a romantic relationship is a part of your safe circle, then enjoy its benefits, take the support that you need and allow your romantic relationship to light up the joy in your life.

Our view of love, dating and relationships has become distorted. We paint an idealistic picture of what the 'right person' looks like — specifically, that they are there to make us feel better about our situation. Or to raise our self-worth, to agree with most of the things that we believe about life and relationships and to always keep us on our toes, excited, invigorated about what the next day looks like, our stomach packed with butterflies. But maybe the right person isn't the one who raises your self-esteem but the one who shows you the mirror. Maybe the right person isn't the one who constantly praises you and puts you on a pedestal but the one who stands beside you and shows you that real life isn't easy, real life isn't all pretty landscapes viewed through a rose-tinted glass, real life isn't having a can-do attitude to <u>all</u> your problems and facing them with every force that you can muster. Real life is coping. It is hurting. Real life is understanding that not every day looks the same, and not every moment is filled with happiness and laughter. Real life is taking one step at a time. It is sometimes being okay and sometimes not but knowing that in both of those moments you're loved. You're cared for. You're cherished by someone other than your blood. That's what the right person brings. That's what the right person can do for you. Maybe the right person was never supposed to transport you to the clouds but to help remove the shackles around your ankles that were stopping you from <u>taking yourself there</u>. The right person was the one that showed you that every day is not going to be an adventure, and some nights will be long and hard, but they will be there to support you. They will be there right beside you. They will be there right beside you.

journal

On your current path to self-love, what would you say you need?

＊ *Alone time.*

＊ *A romantic partner.*

＊ *More romantic dates in your relationship.*

＊ *Some excitement in your sex life/a sex life.*

＊ *Time away from the kids.*

＊ *A few weeks/months/years of being single and discovering who you are.*

HAVING A LACK OF SELF-LOVE CAN HARM YOUR RELATIONSHIP

Maybe you're in a relationship. A long-term or short-term one. Or you're casually dating and haven't planted your roots in anyone's heart yet. Perhaps you're married, with children, or you're planning a family. And now you're on the path to self-love to sustain yourself. To manifest your best life. To make the most of your experiences. To take adventures and enjoy. *You get the gist.*

But until now the lack of self-love in your life harmed your relationship to such an extent that you don't think you're worthy of it anymore. Maybe you want to break it off. You want to walk away after all the damage done. Perhaps you feel that the only way to truly 'love yourself' is to set this person free after the way you may have projected your insecurities on to them.

I'm aware that the situation differs from person to person and breaking this relationship off (if that's the page you're on) can be what's best for you, but for now, put a pin on it, because we will come back to this.

> While the benefits of having the right person by your side are incredible when it comes to loving yourself, it doesn't exclude the possibility of your continuing to witness the dips and dives of life as you keep healing.

The link between self-love and romantic love is strong – we can't deny that. Because a romantic relationship is like any other relationship in your life, and if self-love directly correlates with you having healthy relationships, and that link goes both ways, then a lack of self-love would change the quality of your romantic relationship. In particular, it might inhibit it.

A few ways in which the lack of self-love in one/both partners can poorly affect romantic relationships is through your partner(s):

* *Being unable to develop healthy boundaries.*

* *Being co-dependent.*

* *Being afraid of abandonment.*

* *Creating false perceptions of their partner and relationship.*

* *Projecting their insecurities on to their partner, among others.*

If you have low self-esteem, then those feelings can be projected on to your romantic partner. For example, you find yourself questioning why your partner is with you. What do they see in you? There are so many wonderful people out there, why have they chosen to be with you? You can never match up to how amazing they are – what if they see your imperfections and leave you? Or you feel the need to constantly prove that you're worthy, or you suspect them, projecting your insecurities about your worth on whether they're faithful to you.

Your low self-worth will also show up in the way that you treat them – maybe you push them away when they want to help you, or you isolate yourself from them when the negative self-talk is back, or you pick fights with them because you lean towards the self-fulfilling prophecy that because you don't deserve love, your romantic relationships will always be doomed.

GROW WITH YOUR PARTNER

Looking back at how your relationship has been negatively affected by the lack of self-love in your life can be upsetting, and if your partner treats you well, then it's normal to be guilty over the constant projection of your insecurities on them. But you don't need to end the relationship because of this (as long as you're not toxic for each other). Instead, it should encourage you to include them in your support circle, and to grow with them as you walk on the path to self-love and unlearn all the damaging behaviours you may have displayed.

There is incredible potential in growing with the right person. What I mean by the right person is *the person meant for you*. I mean someone who is good for you. Someone who is healthy for your heart and soothing for your mind. Someone who can transform your life for the better just by being there. By *right person* I mean someone who makes you smile and laugh. Someone who affects you so strongly that their presence still lingers in the air even when you're alone.

There exist people who will easily slip into your life and bring with them a rush of warmth so profound that you won't ever remember feeling cold. People who will hold your hand and it will be as though they are holding your heart instead. People whose one touch will be a balm to all your wounds and – before you know it – you find your scars fading. You find your heart mending. You find your soul smiling. There exist people who can fill your life with so much love that you start to heal without even realising it.

And this doesn't happen as a result of you *depending on them* but as a result of them *being in your life*. Just like those friends who are a part of your safe space, friends who quell your heart and the family that's with you at every step of your healing journey. In the same way, your partner can do so much for you, so include them in your safe space.

In fact, my personal experience forces me to make the following bold statement (say what you will): *the benefits of a **healthy** romantic relationship **far outweigh** the benefits of any non-romantic relationship that you could have. Having the right romantic partner can change your life for the better. So, if you have one, don't let them go.*

My partner Ivnit is this person for me.

It's odd that you can walk through your entire life without knowing that someone exists, but after you speak to them, spend time with them, become friends and fall in love, spending another day without them by your side feels impossible. Love works in wonderfully weird ways. We look at one person and decide that we want to spend the rest of our lives with them, when before we didn't even know where they were or what they were doing. But suddenly, all our dreams now have them by our side, all our hopes for the future entrust them for moral support and all our goals depict them cheering us on with a proud smile on their face. We don't depend on them for our happiness, but we do depend on them to be our biggest support — both mentally and emotionally. We don't build a home inside them but want to build a home together with them. It's odd to think that if we hadn't met them then we'd have continued to go about our journey, unaffected by them. But the moment our paths meet, the moment our destinies collide, the moment we give our heart to them — everything changes forever. And this is why love is so magnificent and so magical. This is why love is the most powerful source in the world. This is why love affects so much in our lives. This is why love exists. This is why.

Think about the two questions below:

Have you struggled with low self-esteem in the past?

Have you ever projected this on to your partner? If so, how? If stuck, refer to the list and examples on page 154.

I want you to note down these behaviours in red. Write them on your mirror, in your journal, in the notes app on your phone and remind yourself that these behaviours are a no-go zone.

For the next month, note down how many times you may project any of these on to your partner.

THE RIGHT PARTNER WILL HELP YOU HEAL

There were many times in my relationship where I was incredibly low. Although I did everything that I could to grow and love myself, my environment – specifically, my dad's addiction to alcohol – had not changed. I didn't remove myself from this environment – *I couldn't* – and instead took it upon myself to be the rescuer whenever something went wrong at home. Many of you who have had parents with addiction will understand. It's difficult to just pack your bags and leave, especially when you have younger siblings or there are other people in the picture who are just as – or more – affected as you. Instead, you stay and be the strong one. The one that makes it through and gives the others courage.

It's not the best decision to make, and many professionals will advise against it, but family relationships work on a different trajectory altogether, and when addiction is involved, it gets complicated. In those moments, the best decision isn't the one that's logical but the one that your heart says to make for those around you. Sometimes self-love is putting others first, even if it's difficult to, because in the long run it will make you happier, and even if it won't, it will give you the satisfaction of knowing that you made a difference in a loved one's life, and that's more than fulfilling, it's more than you could ask for.

For me, being there for my family gave me a sense of purpose, a reason to smile and be happy. But this wasn't always the case. Whenever things went wrong, for example when my dad's alcoholism led him to be hospitalised or brought about other inconvenient situations, I plummeted into darkness. I pushed Ivnit away. I projected my anger on to him. I didn't treat him how he deserved to be treated. This made me feel worse about myself.

I told him that I wasn't worthy of being with him because of all the baggage that I carried. I said that he should find someone who was less of everything that I was. I was embarrassed of my life. Of my family situation. Of my dad's health. Of everything that came along with the years of trauma I had experienced and continued to experience.

But Ivnit never left. He stayed as close as he could. He let me ramble on about my family. He was gentle with my pain. He listened to me when I was low. He let me cry, again and again. He gave me space to grieve, to mend my scars. And he taught me how to move on from my childhood trauma. Whether it was through conversations, a random quote on Instagram or a podcast recommendation, he used whatever means he could to show me that there was a way out. I just had to keep my heart open to it.

Children who grow up in dysfunctional homes struggle as adults with getting into healthy relationships and staying in those relationships. If you're used to chaos, you will look for chaos in your romantic relationship. You will push aside a good partner who comes along and hints at the promise of a better future. You're used to holding on to your darkness. But it's at this point that you should look to the light and welcome the potential of strong, healthy love. It's at this point that you should get out of the dysfunctional cycle that you're in and change your life for the better.

With time I realised how healing my relationship was. It was the healthiest relationship of my life, after all. As someone who'd spent her entire existence being surrounded by arguments, addiction and chaos, I had not seen *'normal'* modelled. And Ivnit showed me this side of love. He brought the calm with him, and my relationship with him gave me a reason to be happy again. It gave me faith. It gave me consolation that even though I couldn't change my upbringing, or the family that came with me, I could change the direction of my future by taking the hand that was held out for me by someone who brought so much light with them.

After getting married and moving in with Ivnit, a new sense of contentment overwhelmed me. The reality that I'd left behind – my childhood home – and would always be drawn back to didn't change. My dad's situation stayed the same, and perhaps it always will. But now I had peace surrounding me, and I felt balanced. I finally felt at ease.

Putting myself first by choosing my relationship and moving away from my childhood home made all the difference in the world. I now had a physical safe space, which was my home. And this was ironic because before this, I spent every day running away from a physical home, where dread washed over me at the thought of going back, because that's how toxic it had become.

Now I was content with my space. I had a group of people around me who were loving and kind. And all this compassion was injected into my heart, which I then extended towards my childhood home and my family within it. Because a part of me would always play the role of rescuer, but it was nice to know that I had someone who supported me along the way.

I don't know what I would've done if I left Ivnit in my darkest moments. I don't know how different my life would be if I'd acted on the thought, *I'm not worthy of this relationship because of my baggage.* Because I was worthy. I had always been worthy. My sight was just muggy with years of childhood trauma.

My relationship with Ivnit showed me that the right person can help you heal in unimaginable ways. You just need to let them in.

Relationships are an integral, vital part of your life. A part that needs to be considered when you walk on the path to self-love in your healing journey. The narrative shouldn't be, 'Loving myself means relying on me, myself and I only,' it should be, 'With others by my side, there's no mountain I can't climb, no battle I can't fight, no trauma I can't face. With others by my side, I can learn to love myself in new ways.'

We project our insecurities in all our relationships when we're in the throes of healing, but we don't suddenly think we're unworthy of being sons, daughters or friends. We don't suddenly think we should cut off our relationship with our parents because we're not in a good place. Instead, we rely on them. We speak to them. We go to *our people* because they are our biggest anchors. So, why do we assume that we're unworthy of being someone's partner, girlfriend, boyfriend, wife or husband after mirroring our insecurities on them?

Why do we not see the truth for what it is: we're in a difficult place, so we should speak to our partners about it rather than isolate ourselves.

> *Our romantic partners are <u>our people</u>, after all,*
> *and they can also be our biggest anchors.*

Relationships differ, and the intricacies of our lives affect how well we function in those relationships. But I'm speaking from my personal experience as someone who has gone through *a hell of a time* and found love while she was healing. I'm speaking as someone who managed to mend the most damaged part of her heart and still find space for a lover, a husband, a life partner. And none of this happened *after I healed*. None of this happened *after I found myself*.

It happened *on* that journey.

It happened as I was living, learning and moving forward.

I fell in love with someone while I was learning to love myself.

Love changes over time and that's the truth. Because how can it stay the same? As you grow older you experience more of the world and witness life in new ways. What 'happiness' means to you changes. What 'growth' means changes. You as a person change. So how could love possibly stay the same? Many people who are lucky to find love in one person are able to grow into this new meaning of love together, but a lot of us don't have that. A lot of us fall in and out of what we thought was love but is nothing other than our trauma staring back at us, and still we refuse to accept a positive and healthy version of love in our lives. That is what's wrong with us. If you're growing into a strong-willed individual, if you've started affirming your worth and if you're changing in considerable ways, then let love change with you. Into something positive. Into something good. Don't let the other aspects of your life grow with you while you still see love as that fragile, tender thing that caused you so much pain in the past. The good thing about love growing with you is this — as everything else in your life falls into place, love does too.

Firstly, there is *no end* to finding yourself. Tell me, will you ever stop growing? As long you keep living, meeting new people, stepping out of your city, comfort zone or home, you will keep changing. You will keep learning. You will keep uncovering new personality traits. You can't discover who you are when that 'you' is constantly evolving. So, when this idea that you will reach the end point and 'find yourself' goes out the window, so does the assumption that you *should wait* until that point to get into a romantic relationship. There's no waiting. There's just falling. In love. With your person.

Secondly, even while being in a relationship, you can be high and low in your healing. You can still have down days. You can still drown in self-neglect. You can be super content one day and completely empty another. And that is okay. Having down days, churning in negative thoughts or feeling bad about yourself doesn't mean that you must break up with your partner. It doesn't mean that you must distance yourself from them – unless that will help you. It doesn't mean that suddenly you're unworthy of them because you're in a dark place in your healing.

It just means that you're human, and you get to be human together.

> If you're on the path to self-love and have projected your past trauma on to the people around you, including your romantic partner, take a breather. Sit them down and explain what's going on in your mind. If they love you, they will understand. They will want to help you. They will encourage you to walk on this self-love journey and when you come out the other side, they will be there, cheering for you.

The purpose of the path to self-love isn't to change yourself overnight. The purpose is to acknowledge where your negative patterns of behaviour come from, and to work towards unlearning them. One way of doing this is engaging in honest communication with your partner. Tell them what you're up to. Encourage them to helpfully point out the next time you act in an unkind way. Together, you can walk towards the path to self-love and make the most of your relationships

Sometimes you will have low days. Sometimes self-neglect will coil in your stomach. And other times you will have the adventure of a lifetime and love that you have someone to share it with. Don't deny yourself that. Don't push the people that love you away when you're 'finding yourself'.

exercise

Let's go back to the start of this section (page 153) where we considered those of you in a relationship who have struggled with low self-esteem and self-worth and haven't been able to practise self-love in the recent past.

As a result, you have projected your insecurities and don't know whether to break off your relationship or stay.

Ask yourself whether you want to stay in the relationship. Here are a few ways to figure that out:

✳ *Does your partner make you happy and fulfil your needs?*

✳ *Do they respect you?*

❋   *Have the projections of your low self-worth been unprovoked?*

❋   *Does your partner create a safe environment for you to express your thoughts?*

❋   *Do you believe the relationship is redeemable?*

One part of having low self-esteem is always blaming yourself for things that go wrong, even when it isn't your fault.

It can be the case that a lot of your projection isn't actually unwarranted and is in fact a consequence of the way your partner has acted.

In such cases, the best way forward is to sit down and have an honest conversation with them.

Talk about what's gone wrong until now and what to do next. You might need couples therapy. You might need to take a few steps back in your relationship. You both need to be honest and take accountability, because while they may have worries that are brought on by your projection, you're allowed to have worries too.

The right love will come, the one that beats all the others. The love that leaves a smile on your face that stretches from cheek to cheek and doesn't fade even as the day turns grey. The love that teaches you how beautiful you are even when you don't feel it, even when you pull and tug at all your flaws, it looks at you through half-lidded eyes that admire you in your entirety. The love that appreciates how hard you try, even when your heart is heavy because life hasn't been too kind, even when you're anxious or scared about what the future holds. The love that makes you feel soft with warmth and affection, the love that tries hard to make you smile and never leaves your side. The love that recognises your need to be alone but to also have them by your side, supporting you, encouraging you to be better and work harder and become stronger along the way. The love that doesn't go to sleep until it knows that you're okay, the love that understands all your emotions, your mood swings, your insecurities and your vulnerabilities that you try so hard to hide but are unable to. The right love will come. The love that accepts you completely, even on days when you can't accept yourself and feel lost and alone, and even on nights when you don't know how to go on.

If you're in a relationship, how has your relationship with your partner helped you in your healing journey?

DON'T LOOK FOR LOVE FOR THE WRONG REASONS

If everything that I've said so far has reaffirmed your decision to stay in your relationship, or keep your heart open to love, then that's great. But if it's encouraged you to look for love with the hope that *it will heal you* on your journey, then that's misguided. Your path to self-love is yours and yours only. On this path, if you find love, great, good for you, that adds one more person to your support circle. But if you don't, that's fine too.

Because it means that you can learn to be comfortable alone and continue enjoying your single life, making the most of what you like to do. It means that you can discover self-love and practise it without worrying about how it will affect your romantic partner. For example, if you want to go on a silent meditation retreat for two months, you can pack up your bags and go without having to worry about leaving your husband or wife behind. Of course, if you're with someone, you could always take them with you, but the point is that if you're single, you don't have to think about these things in the same way.

If you're on the path to self-love, your aim should not be to find romantic love but to find ways in which you can walk on this path alone, because a relationship can't save you if you're drowning. Romantic love can be a great source of happiness and excitement, but you still need to be on your own path to self-discovery and healing. You still need to be your own person.

Before Ivnit and I started dating, I knew what I had to do to work on my health and happiness, and I was practising self-love for years before him. In many ways Ivnit was a token of strength for me; his dedication to all areas of his life encouraged me to refocus my energy on what mattered instead of losing sight of who I was. But in other ways Ivnit reminded me what I'd known all along. He reignited my faith in myself, and in my ability to manifest my happiness.

After many years of being with Ivnit, I know that healing from trauma, finding yourself and being in a relationship are all compatible. But I've also understood the invaluable gift of spending time with myself, of being my own person. I know how to be comfortable in my own company. I know how to be *me without him.*

The bottom line is, if you're also looking for love when you're on the path to self-love, then *let it come to you.* While the universe works its magic, make sure that you're practising both easy and tough self-love to evolve and be happier in your own presence, and go ahead and manifest all those positive things that you see lifting your life. Whether it's journalling, or writing it on a mirror, or recording it to listen back later – manifest love and light in your life the way that you deem fit.

Then wait for the universe to send what is meant for you, to you. Because manifestation magic *is real*, and it is beautiful.

> Manifestation and energies might seem mysterious, but the idea can be put simply in the following terms: <u>if you think positive, then positive things will happen to you</u>.

But don't stand still. Don't wait for love to slip into your life and fix you, because a romantic partner can't mend your scars or put your broken pieces back together – only you can. Remember, the people who love you are there to support you and provide you with comfort and joy. So, if what you're waiting for is to be saved by a romantic partner, then find ways to save yourself. Keep walking on this road that you're on. Make use of those who are already in your safe space. And remember that no matter who comes into your life, your most important relationship is the one that you have with yourself, and your healing is dependent on how well you can manage that relationship.

So, work on what's on the inside, and the outside will fall into place.

There are so many benefits to becoming self-dependent, to becoming comfortable in your own presence and learning the importance of solitude. One of the actions that truly changed my life forever was spending time with myself with just my thoughts for company. In the beginning it was uncomfortable, my mind a battleground of grey cloudy thoughts that refused to align. But the more time that I spent with myself, the more I understood that it was never about bringing my conflicting thoughts together but about learning where they came from, figuring out if there was a way that I could deal with the negative ones and moving forward with them, not without them. These days I go on a daily walk, and even if I don't have to clear my head — which is highly unlikely, as there is so much for me to figure out — I still benefit from the walks. I try to get some sunshine, as much sun as muggy London allows, I read a self-help book and I spend time with myself. It is so, so healing. To be alone. To be your own best friend. To rely on yourself for things that you would historically have relied on others for. Because now I don't need to wait if I want to go on a walk, or go shopping, or go to a spa. I just go. Now I don't need to wait if I want to watch a movie. Now, I just grab my keys and leave. Now I just enjoy life the way that I was always supposed to. And that is so, so freeing.

chapter 6

boundaries

Boundaries are the golden key when unlocking self-love. They help you to protect yourself, as well as those around you, allowing you to maintain healthy, wholesome relationships with those who are in your support circle, and they help you manage your priorities and avoid situations that cause you discomfort. Through boundary-setting, you create a nourishing external environment through which you can cultivate happiness, conquer your daily challenges and ensure that your relationships are thriving.

> Self-love is about improving the quality of your life, and sometimes this involves doing things that are difficult to do, such as boundary-setting. Boundaries are used not just to maintain healthy relationships but to save those relationships that are at risk of falling apart.

But why do we need to set boundaries to save our relationships? We've had conversations about relationships. Hefty, long, engaging conversations which have drawn a link between self-love and nurturing relationships, and during these conversations, it became clear that while having a safe support circle is beneficial, there can come a point in your life when someone close to you acts in a way that harms your mental and emotional well-being.

We saw this in Chapter Three (page 67), where the people you love can hurt you, and although in cases of strong emotional abuse you should cut them out of your life, in cases of subtle emotional abuse the relationship can be redeemable. And one core element of redeeming a cracked relationship is setting healthy boundaries.

This was also mentioned in Chapter Five (page 123), where we spoke about support circles and removing toxic people. Sometimes people aren't entirely toxic for you, and in these cases the relationship is, once again, redeemable. In fact, the person could be so important to you that you need them in your safe space – only then can you continue practising self-love and living your best life. For this reason, you need a way to save the relationship, and again this is where boundaries come in.

Sometimes a relationship doesn't need saving, but boundaries are still important. Boundaries are a form of tough self-love, as setting your boundaries and expectations can take a lot out of you. But it's something that you do to ensure that your relationships don't fall apart down the line. In fact, it's advisable that you set boundaries at the start of your relationships so that there are no surprises, and no one gets hurt later because they didn't know where you stood in relation to each other.

Through boundary-setting you can reap the benefits of your relationships and grow together, continuing to seek your goals, your peace and a bright future.

Boundaries can do wonders to keep your relationships from falling apart. I have friends who I might have lost, had I not put boundaries in place. By creating boundaries, I've kept people in my life close but also protected myself from giving too much to others and too little to myself.

Be vocal about your boundaries but accept that boundaries and respect work both ways. Be a good listener, be a loyal and trusting friend. Understand that apologising doesn't make you any less worthy. Be honest about your own feelings towards others and your experiences. Be kind and gentle with others — you don't always know what your loved ones are going through. Learn to trust others. Forgive them. Don't badmouth those that you love — once those words have left your mouth, they can't be taken back. Remember to affirm their achievements and joy — sharing your happiness with your loved ones is so much more fulfilling than enjoying it alone. Understand that effort should be balanced between two people. Don't ask for too much of other people and don't let them ask for too much of you.

What Are Boundaries?

> **Boundary: A Definition**
> *A boundary is a line standing between you and another person, a line that – if you're the one that's drawing it – the person standing opposite can't cross. Boundaries are fluid and can change over time. The same boundary could also mean different things to people depending on their values and worldview.*

There are many boundaries that you can set, and they fall under the following categories:

* **Physical boundaries** – *This is about your physical space, e.g. how close you're willing to stand next to someone, whether you're comfortable in hugging them or shaking their hand, as well as the sexual boundaries that you set in your romantic relationship.*

* **Time boundaries** – *This is about your time and how you like to spend it, e.g. giving your friend one hour on the weekend for coffee, or four for lunch and a walk, and expecting this to be respected.*

* **Emotional boundaries** – *This is about your emotional health, e.g. if you're okay with watching a movie about death while grieving or celebrating your friend's engagement after experiencing a heartbreak yourself.*

* **Intellectual boundaries** – *This is about your worldview, i.e. refraining from having a conversation with someone who*

holds strong misogynistic or racist views, or being vocal about what your moral standpoint is in such cases.

✳ ***Material boundaries*** *– This is about material possessions that are of value to you, e.g. how much money you're willing to lend someone, or whether you're comfortable in sharing your clothes/materialistic possessions with others.*

Although boundaries shouldn't be crossed, they are fluid and can change over time depending on what your wants and needs are. Imagine you're an 18-year-old socially anxious teenager who has just started university and you meet your extrovert flatmate. You're a little uncomfortable when they ask you to go flat party hopping. You decide to give it a try but hate it and raise it with your flatmate. At this point you set a boundary by telling them that you would rather spend your nights at one party, in a quiet bar or at home. If your flatmate enjoys your company, then they will respect your boundary and join you, but if they want to spend the night meeting new people, then they can say no and go without you.

It's important to note that your friend hasn't crossed your boundary by telling you that they're going without you – this boundary would only be crossed if they *forced you* or peer-pressured you into joining them despite your saying no. The response that they give you is important as it shows what their priorities are, and although boundaries are a good way to demonstrate to others where they stand in relation to you, they are also a great way to see where you stand in relation to them.

You will see what your flatmate's boundary is on this occasion. Maybe they are okay with toning down their extrovert personality for an evening, but speaking to new people and partying gives them life – and they can't change who they are for you. They won't have a good time in a quiet bar or one flat party. As a result, them going without you would be them, in turn, *setting their boundary* for you. This boundary would show that there are certain things that you can expect from them, i.e., having easy banter and a laugh, but certain things that you can't, i.e., denying them the opportunity of making new friends and having fun.

Now, imagine this boundary of yours changes over time. A few months have passed, and you have a brand-new circle of friends (including your original flatmate) who you're happy with. One Saturday night, your friends attend a few flat parties. Being around this group puts you at ease and you feel as though you can conquer anything when they are by your side. So, on this night you're confident and decide to join them as they go flat party hopping. Does this mean that your first boundary was uncalled for? No, it doesn't. It means that your circumstances have changed, and because of that, so have your boundaries. There are things that you're now comfortable with doing in a group that you weren't okay doing with just one friend. A good friend understands this change and commends you for embracing new adventures and growing with time.

Boundaries are fluid, so they can be moved, as well as replaced by new boundaries as you grow with your experiences. This is important when you're on the path to self-love, as who you become as you go through that journey won't be the same as who you were at the start, and as a result the boundaries that you set, and your expectations of others, will change.

Bear this in mind when you're setting boundaries in your relationships.

What you need at the start of your healing journey may not be what you need as you continue walking on that path.

journal

Have you set a boundary recently?

If yes, was this a physical, emotional, intellectual, time or material possession boundary?

How did this go? Write it in as much detail as possible.

If you were to set this boundary again, would you do anything differently?

How Can Boundaries Help My Relationships?

I've known Sonia for a while, and it was only in the last few years that I noticed she never seemed to have money when we went out. Initially when we'd plan to meet up, I'd receive a message from Sonia a day or two before along the lines of, 'Can we cancel this week? I'm a little broke and can't afford dinner.' But I really wanted to see her, so I did the first thing that came to my mind – I'd offer to pay for her. 'It's okay,' I'd tap away on my phone, 'this time, dinner is on me.'

Other times, Sonia wouldn't even cancel and would start complaining about how broke she was as we made our way to the restaurant, and this would induce feelings of guilt on my part. As a result, I'd automatically extend my card to the waiter when it was time to pay the bill, brushing off Sonia's advances with a 'Don't worry about it. You can pay for the next dinner.' But that would never happen.

Sonia had a full-time job, and I was working part-time while struggling to pursue my dream of being an author. This meant that at the end of each month Sonia's income was guaranteed, while I struggled to get by and had to manage my finances carefully. I found myself in this position on several occasions, and eventually I noticed the pattern and felt very uncomfortable with it. Over time I also noticed that when we met, Sonia would show me the new designer bag she recently bought or I'd notice her freshly painted acrylics, or she would talk about a holiday that she'd booked, and in the same conversation she would complain about how broke she was.

It dawned on me that Sonia didn't value money in the same way that I did.

Getting her nails done or buying a new designer bag were high on her list of priorities, but paying off her loan or setting aside money for our dinner dates weren't. And in buying her dinner every so often, I was fuelling her disordered priorities and affirming what she was doing. In paying for her I was also giving her too much of my time, effort and – particularly – money. Money that I didn't owe her a penny of. This affected my feelings towards our friendship. Before this realisation hit me, I was very happy with her and looked forward to our meetups, but the more that I noticed this pattern, the less I wanted to see her. Without realising it, I started putting off our dates for months at a time, and it was only later that it occurred to me that it was because of this subconscious ick that I developed towards her, and she had no idea.

So, what did I do about it? I formed boundaries.

Instead of offering to pay for her, I offered her an alternative. If she messaged me saying that she was too broke for dinner, I responded with, 'To be honest, me too. I've paid for too much this month. Do you think you have enough for coffee? If not, we can meet another time.' Usually she would respond earnestly, perhaps she was relieved that I was in the same place as her, and a few times she suggested that I go over to hers for coffee.

This was great because it meant that I could spend time with her without the sourness of feeling used by someone I considered a dear friend.

> Setting boundaries doesn't need to be confrontational. You can set an expectation with a slight nod of the head, with the way that you position your body, with the words that you use that gently convey your thoughts.

Notice that this boundary was subtle. I didn't directly say, 'This is what you're doing and I'm not okay with it.' I just drew a thin line using my communication. I didn't want to offend her by pointing out that I had paid for her on many occasions, because there were several things that she had done for me throughout the years which I perhaps hadn't done for her, things that were more valuable than money. But the constant dinner-paying *was affecting me*, so I wanted to put a stop to it, and I wanted to do it without damaging her self-respect.

As a result of this boundary, I felt better about us meeting up. Over time she didn't mention being broke as much as she did before, and whenever she did mention it, I countered it with a similar response to the above, so she got the point – I wasn't paying for her. We could now both enjoy each other's company without feeling bad about it, because I'm sure that me paying for her on all those meet-ups must have been hard on her too. It also meant that I didn't have to cut off a friend whose company I enjoy, a friend who adds value to my life in all other ways.

Setting this boundary has made me feel safer in our friendship, and I no longer believe that I'm giving and giving without getting anything in return. And this is what boundaries can do for you – they can help you out of uncomfortable situations with your loved ones that aren't relationship-ending-worthy but still don't sit right with you. Situations where you would rather avoid confrontation and instead iron out any creases in your relationship in a different way. At the end of it, a better relationship means a happier you!

Boundaries allow you to keep those who make you happy in your support circle and fix problems without things getting messy.

Setting boundaries doesn't need to be confrontational, it doesn't even need to be overtly expressed. It can be subtle, it can be in the way that you hold yourself, in your communication, in the distance that you draw between yourself and others. For example, when setting a physical boundary, you can easily show someone that you're not comfortable with hugging them by either extending your hand or nodding your head at them instead. You don't need to say a word. Remember, setting these boundaries is a way to protect yourself. It's a way to put your needs and wants first without offending others because you don't want to create an uncomfortable environment for yourself either.

People are often quite good at picking up social cues, so if you respond to their behaviour with a physical, communicative or emotional block of your own, they should get the point. But what if they don't get the point? And what if they do and they don't respect your boundaries?

How to deal with conflict: tell the other person, 'I understand that your perspective is different to mine, and I respect your opinion, but I don't agree with it.' Try to limit your contact with the person causing you discomfort. If you both belong to the same circle of friends, or are from the same family, make plans with your loved ones individually, rather than as a group. Don't stoop to their level if they talk badly about you. If anyone asks you what happened, be honest about it but don't put others in a position where they have to pick a side. If you're unable to find a solution to this problem, then cut off all contact — you're better off not having them in your life rather than being anxious every time you're around them. Draw your boundaries with people. Don't let them treat you wrongly and don't let yourself be swayed by other people's expectations of you. Respect your relationships but remember to respect yourself just as much.

When people don't respect your boundaries, you can feel hurt. Misunderstood. You can even feel regret because they've gaslit you or guilt-tripped you into believing that your feelings are unjustified. On those occasions where you have tried but failed to create balance in your relationship, ask yourself whether this person's presence in your life is good for you, just as you would when you're deciding who should be in your safe space. If the answer is no, then now is the time to let them go. People aren't meant to be in your life forever and often letting go of them is more healing than keeping them.

Remember, setting boundaries is a way for you to save your relationships – but only if the other person is willing to listen. Boundaries can't glue together broken relationships or repair toxic ones, or fix relationships with those who don't care about keeping you enough to mend their ways for you.

Secondly, boundaries only work if you're both on the same page. If you have different worldviews or a conflicting moral standpoint, then it's tricky to get the other person to meet you where you need them, and to be honest, you can't expect it of them either. In these situations, it's better to let go of those people than to keep them in your life. Just like forming boundaries is an act of self-love, so is letting go.

> Sometimes setting boundaries happens out in the open. Instead of being subtle about it, you're clear and put your expectations across, because that's the only way that you can set this boundary. And this method of boundary-setting is more likely to result in conflict or a broken relationship.

One time, I had to set a boundary with my friend, Hannah. I noticed that she was badmouthing a friend of ours and I didn't appreciate this. I could've turned the other way and not made a comment, but my morals didn't allow me to let this happen behind my friend's back. Initially, I didn't tell Hannah off or directly voice that she was doing something wrong. Instead, I said, 'We shouldn't speak about our friends behind their backs.'

This didn't go well. Hannah denied her actions. I then firmly set my boundary and told her that what she did was wrong, and I didn't appreciate it. The conversation ended on a bitter note, and Hannah didn't change her behaviour and continued badmouthing our friend. A few weeks later, I again made my boundaries clear with Hannah – talking about your friends behind their backs was unacceptable. But she still refused to apologise for her actions, or even acknowledge the wrongness of them. I realised then that our worldviews were very different, and we wouldn't see eye-to-eye on matters such as this.

For this reason, I cut Hannah from my safe space forever.

This wasn't easy for me, because Hannah had become a valuable friend over the years. She was hilarious and cheered me up when I was low. But after spending more alone time together, I'd noticed this personality trait of hers, where she often badmouthed and criticised people. This was a flaw of hers, one that outweighed all the positives of us sharing a friendship.

Now, everyone has flaws. I'm not perfect either and I have many traits that can make others uncomfortable. But I can still be flawed and loved, just like you can, because the people who love us are able to despite our shortcomings. They don't mind our flaws. Our flaws don't contradict their moral values. Our flaws don't make them uncomfortable, or if they do, then they can overlook this because our positive traits outweigh our negative ones. But I couldn't love Hannah despite her flaws because they contradicted my values.

If you've noticed a mismatch in your relationship – perhaps you feel uncomfortable or unhappy with that person, or you've noticed a personality trait that you don't like – then the first step is to set a boundary or two. If the other person refuses to respect this boundary, then consider whether the flaws in the relationship (or in them) can be overlooked. Can you love them despite their imperfections, or are these imperfections causing you discomfort? Can you accept them with open arms despite their flaws conflicting with your moral values, or would having them in your life hinder your positive journey? These are questions to ask yourself when someone you care about doesn't respect your boundaries.

Remember, if someone doesn't respect your boundaries – those that you introduced because you don't want to cut them off entirely – then think about whether you want to continue having them in your life. Also consider whether them continuing to be in your life – after ignoring your boundaries and causing a bitter aftertaste in your friendship – will contribute to your life in any positive way.

> Your support circle is sacred. If you keep making excuses for those who step all over your boundaries, then forget about self-love and healing – you will lose who you are in the process of keeping them.

Letting people go can sometimes feel like you're letting yourself go. You hand others pieces of you in the process of finding yourself — but when those relationships fall apart, you feel like you've lost a part of yourself. You feel like you've lost a sense of who you are. Letting people go is like unlearning everything that you knew about yourself in the months and years that you knew them, and it's hard. Believe me, it is so damn hard. But nothing stays the same. Not our relationships. Not the love we hold for others. Nor the people we become. So, believing that we must hold on to others forever isn't right. Because everyone comes into your life when they're supposed to, and they leave when the lesson you had to learn, or the adventure you were destined to take, has happened. And that's all. And I know that it's hard to accept this truth, it's difficult to tell yourself that this person leaving is something that you can live with, something that you have to live with. But you have the strength to deal with a lot more than a few losses — trust me. And sure, maybe you will lose a part of yourself when they leave, but maybe, just maybe, those gaps will make room for new parts, new lessons and new adventures just waiting to happen to you.

exercise

Earlier you were encouraged to write down if you'd set any boundaries in place.

I now want you to write what matters to you when you think of the following boundaries: physical, time, emotional, intellectual, material. E.g., 'I'm not comfortable with hugging strangers,' or 'I don't give more than one hour a week to phone calls with my mum,' or 'I'm up for casual dating but can't commit emotionally.'

Now it's time to apply these boundaries.

Start by saying them in a negative way: 'No, I don't want to go to the theatre.' 'No, I don't have time to meet for coffee.' 'No, I don't want to lend you my Prada bag.'

Now, turn these into a positive. 'I won't be able to make it to the theatre, but you go ahead and enjoy yourself.' 'I'm a little busy this week. How about I let you know a time that works for me in the next few weeks?' 'That bag is my favourite, I'd hate for anything to happen to it. You can borrow a different bag, or we can go shopping and get you a new one?'

Remember, when setting boundaries, you can very easily hurt those that you love, and that's not an ideal situation to be in, especially if that person matters to you. Next time someone is seen as a threat to your boundary, use safe, kind communication and draw the line where necessary.

Positive communication will allow you to not only set your boundary and protect yourself but also to protect your relationship. But sometimes you will need to be firm. Sometimes you will need to show others where they stand with you, and that is okay. Self-love requires you to put those who treat you wrongly in their place.

If boundary-setting doesn't work, then you know what the final decision to make is. Leave, cut them off and put yourself first.

chapter 7

balancing loving yourself with loving others

When we think of self-love, we think of creating a healthy relationship with ourselves. Most people think self-love is about them, and no one else, and before picking up this book, you might have thought the same. But this is far from the truth.

The problem is that we've forgotten about other people entirely when we engage in self-love activities. These activities, specifically the ones we see on social media, are focused on ourselves; there's so much emphasis on being independent, on relying only on yourself for long-lasting happiness, that other people – those who need you and rely on you – look like a threat. Other people look like the enemy to self-love. But they're not. Your loved ones are a part of your self-love journey.

Even if it is about you, you're not detached from the external world. Your relationships, the people you interact with, your job, your failures and achievements – these all contribute to the person that you become. The way you practise self-love will affect others, and your practice will be influenced by them. To flourish in your self-love journey, you must strike a balance between the relationship you share with yourself and the relationship you share with others.

You need other people to live a fulfilling life.
For this reason, if you keep putting yourself
first at the cost of their welfare, then
you're harming these nourishing relationships,
which will — in turn — harm your quality
of life down the line.

Are your relationships with others balanced? Maybe you don't give enough to others?

Is your relationship with yourself balanced? Maybe you feel you give too much of yourself away to others?

Things I struggle with: believing that it's okay to say '_no_' to someone, even if it means hurting their feelings. I struggle with accepting that people can love me for me, and I don't need to do anything further, or be anyone else, or mould myself into their expectations of me. Others _love me for me_. Just as I am, and nothing more. I struggle with feeling guilty whenever I put myself first. I've been accustomed to putting others first so often that it seems wrong somehow to do something for myself before I do it for them. And I find it hard to ask for favours or help from others. I struggle with asking for the same favours that other people will easily demand or expect from me. I also find it hard to believe that there exist people who love you and care about you, and who will be there for you without the slightest expectation that you do anything more, or extra, for them in return. I've spent so long with half-hearted individuals with little to no regard for me that I struggle with accepting that those who love you will always love you and be there for you, asking for nothing other than love and respect in return. Those who care about you want nothing more than your happiness. Those who love you just love you. And that's it.

Why Do We Need Balance?

Our culture and social media perpetuate a 'me, me, me' mindset, which has resulted in people seeing self-love as at odds with the love we can offer other people.

There needs to be a healthy balance between how much you show up for others and how much you show up for yourself.

People often struggle with knowing when to put others first. Some of you prioritise those around you to such an extent that you forget about yourself entirely. You think about, empathise with and feel too much for your loved ones, bending yourselves backwards to make sure they're happy. Although you can bring lots of joy to those around you and benefit from those relationships, you do this at the cost of your own well-being. This hasn't proven useful in your own road to happiness, and instead it causes you dissatisfaction, because not only are you sacrificing what's good for you to make others happy, but you're also constantly guilt-ridden that you don't do enough for your loved ones – *no matter how much you do.*

Some of you have noticed this pattern and can see how damaging it is, so you have strayed in the opposite direction; you refuse to let others walk all over you, and you stop putting others first at the cost of your own well-being. You're not afraid to ask for what you deserve, and that's commendable. You can confidently point out when you've been treated poorly or taken for granted, and you can put your foot down because you reflect on how others can harm your mental health. You can also be sensitive to people's emotions and needs and can understand how others can be hurt by your actions – but the problem is, you won't always do something about this.

Neither of these approaches have the right balance. The first results in too much self-sacrifice, where you're giving your valuable time, effort and love for next to nothing in return, and the second is too self-centred. Seeking this kind of independence can cause you to become hyper-independent, where you end up putting other people at the bottom of your list of priorities, with your mental, emotional and physical health taking precedence in all cases, because you falsely believe that you *don't need people* for your self-love journey.

> Hyper-independence is an extreme form of relying on yourself and refusing to look to others for support. This causes you to struggle to form long-term relationships and benefit from engaging in healthy ones which have the potential to bring joy, adventure and peace in your life.

What people practising this kind of self-love fail to understand is that putting their mental, emotional and physical health first *includes* their relationships. You can't put yourself first without considering the people around you.

When you've had a long week, you might think, 'I really need to meet my girls and unwind this weekend,' or 'I miss my family, I'll call Mum and have a catch-up. I can go over for tea if she's home.' When you take your dog to the park, you ask your neighbour to come along because you enjoy his hilarious gossip. When you go to a yoga class, you remember that your sister wanted to go too, so you take her with you. When you see the trailer for a new movie, you know your partner would love it, so you include it in next week's date night.

These are all forms of self-care that improve your mental, emotional and physical health, but also take other people into consideration.

You can do all these activities by yourself, but sharing these experiences with others adds value for you. The people who love and care about you can bring you so much joy. Spending time with others, giving them your time, being there for them, offloading or having a laugh and forgetting your problems for a while are some of the beautiful jewels of having good relationships. These relationships bring meaning to your life and contribute to your self-love journey.

> Sharing your safe space with others and being
> a part of their space is the key to healing and
> living a comfortable life.

Having a safe circle with kind and compassionate humans is so important, but you have a significant part to play in keeping these relationships nurturing and good too, as relationships work both ways. When practising self-love, keep those who are good to you close to you, but make sure that you're good to them too. You can do this by being there for others when they need you and not letting them down. You can do this by sharing a part of your life, your emotions and your love with them. You can do this by putting them first when it will help them. And these actions raise your quality of life too, because being surrounded by warm, happy people will help keep you happy. Striking the near-perfect balance between these two sides of your life will create harmony in all other areas of your life too.

We spend so long living like we are the main character of our stories that we forget that we can also teach other people lessons. Invaluable lessons. Lessons that help them grow. Lessons that show them what it means to love and value someone else. What it means to put others first. What it means to take care of yourself, but not at the expense of others. Sometimes we can be the hurdle someone else needs to cross. Sometimes we can be the light in their life, or a regret. A hard to swallow regret. A regret that can either stay with them forever or be nothing other than a stepping-stone in their journey. The point is sometimes they need to be taught something about life and we are the tool for them to get there. We are the reason they change, the reason they become better versions of themselves or learn to value themselves more. We are the light. Or the darkness. Their happiness and their pain. We are the shackles that tie them to their past or the wings on their back that finally teach them how to fly.

POSITIVE ENERGIES EVERYWHERE

Another reason this balance is important is that other people's moods can affect your mood. As social beings, we pick up on other people's energies, especially those around us: our colleagues, family, friends, romantic partners. If you go to work and your colleague is having a bad day, their negative energy will rub off on you after hours of them moping about their own problems. In the same way, when those that you love are in a great mood, you naturally adopt that great mood too – like when you see your friends after a long week and they are bursting with positive energy, making you feel lighter too.

If you love yourself, sure, do what's best for you, but if you do this without any consideration for someone else's well-being, then you're using self-love to only your own benefit, which is wrong.

For this reason, you have a responsibility to keep those around you happy, to make sure that you're a good friend, partner, daughter, son, parent. Because while your friend's energy has the power to affect yours, your energy can affect them too. For instance, if your friend is going through a heartbreak, hearing about it might bring you down, reminding you of your own experience, but you have the power to change their mood and allow them to see the brighter side through your words of encouragement and by being there for them. You can take your friend on a walk, treat them to dessert or just let them offload, and this does wonders for a grieving heart. Not only will your friend feel lighter after spending time with you, but you will also feel better about yourself – because bringing your loved ones joy will fulfil you. You will feel better about yourself.

Of course, sometimes it's not even about cheering your friend up and leaving them feeling better but just being there for them. Not being okay is fine too, but as social beings we can take comfort in each other's presence, even in times of hardship. Even if you can't cheer them up, being there for those that you love and just giving them a listening ear can fill you with a sense of purpose. This contributes to your feelings of worthiness and can often motivate you to conquer your own challenges too, such as practising self-love on a tough and tedious healing journey.

journal

When was the last time you saw a friend who was going through something? How did this make you feel?

Did you manage to make them feel better or lighter in any way? How did this make you feel?

How Do I Balance Loving Myself with Loving Others?

Imagine you had a long day at work and were expected to meet up with your friend, but you couldn't bring yourself to do it, so you cancelled on them last minute. This caused your friend's mood to fall, and you noticed this low mood through their text messages or the tone of their voice. This made you feel guilty about cancelling on them, and an exhausting day at work ended with a guilt-ridden and dull evening at home, where you mindlessly scrolled on social media and felt even more zombie-like than before. In this situation, not only did you miss the opportunity to unwind and offload to *your person* after an exhausting eight hours of being micro-managed by your passive-aggressive boss, but you also brought your friend's energy down who was looking forward to seeing you.

Even if you didn't have the drive to see your friend, it's possible that going to see them could have invigorated you more than heading home and spending hours scrolling through your phone.

But what if you were *really* exhausted, or had a horrible day? Surely you can't force yourself to step out. This is true, and in situations like this it's okay to cancel on your friend – but explain to them how you're feeling. You never know, they might notice that something is wrong and offer to come over with a tub of ice cream or your favourite takeaway.

Tell me, how many times have you wanted to cancel a plan with your friends but gone to see them anyway, and afterwards you felt so energised and happy, and relieved that you didn't cancel last minute because of exhaustion or low mood? I've experienced this countess times, and now I don't ever pull out of plans to see those who I'm confident will lift my vibration. And I don't make plans with people that I know I won't want to see closer to the event. What's the point of letting someone down when I had no intention of committing to the plan to begin with? The best decision is to make plans with people who will make you happy, so you never think twice about meeting them when the plan gets closer. And even if you do want to cancel, you feel comfortable enough to tell them why.

> When I first started practising what I thought was self-love, I'd cancel on my friends on the regular because I was putting <u>my needs</u> first. This not only negatively affected my relationships, but it also made me incredibly lonely. Because my friends, who I was harming with my constant flaking, set their own boundaries to put themselves first.

So, how do you do it? How do you know when it's okay to cancel on someone after an exhausting day and when it isn't? Because either way you will hurt those who are close to you, so when is it justified?

The path to self-love doesn't stipulate that you can never hurt those around you, because that's impossible, especially when you're putting yourself first after a long time of not thinking about yourself at all. These new actions can be a shock to many who have always relied on you and even take you for granted.

If you've always said yes to your friend for coffee on Fridays, even though you would rather spend your evening idling on the sofa, and now as part of your self-love journey you're giving yourself Fridays off so you can reflect on the week, your friend will be surprised by this. They might be hurt, and even feel let down. But that's okay. Because it's not your job to show up for everyone all the time, especially at the cost of your own happiness. It's your job to show up for others when it will make the most difference to their life, and when it won't necessarily affect yours. In this situation, you can be more present for your friend on a Saturday, after a well-rested night, or on a Sunday when you've done all your chores. So, offer this day instead. Tell them that you're not up for your Friday meetups anymore because this is a part of your new self-love journey. If your friend loves you, they will understand. In fact, they might even encourage you to put yourself first.

But if your friend is horrified by this and calls you out for putting yourself first, then question where the balance lies in your relationship. Do they turn up for you as well? Do they listen to you and respect your thoughts? Or have they started taking you for granted? This would be an ideal time to set boundaries in your relationship. The beautiful thing about all these actions is that they're all related. Improving one aspect of your life will encourage you to assess another and fix that too.

Try the following when balancing your relationship with others and your relationship with yourself:

* *When you're committing to your friend for something, assess whether it will do any of the following:*

  * *Harm your well-being*

  * *Put you in a difficult position*

  * *Exhaust you further*

  * *Bring you unhappiness*

* *When showing up for your friends, think about how much of yourself you're giving the other person; an evening out after*

a long day is manageable, but saying yes to the next ten Sundays to plan a bridal shower can be very taxing.

✳ *If you say no, will you be harming your loved one in any way? E.g., if they've had a heartbreak and are at the brink of breakdown, not going to see them will hurt them even more. It's a delicate time.*

✳ *Ask yourself whether you're doing more for them than they're doing for you as a whole? A near-balanced friendship lasts longer than an imbalanced one.*

exercise

Think about what you do for others and how much this takes out of you.

If you were to show up for your loved ones, would you do anything different to what you do now?

For the next week, try and strike a balance between how many self-love activities you engage in and how many activities you take part in for others.

Remember, these can overlap, as often what you do for others makes you happy too, and some of your self-love activities can be done together.

Strike two goals with one ball!

Sometimes you don't have the strength to see others or be there for them. You just don't. And putting yourself in an uncomfortable position isn't right, especially if you've had a long day, or if you're in the throes of a difficult healing journey which makes it hard to step out of bed, let alone go to see someone. A lot of the time this can be the case with people who cancel plans last minute, or make plans and never follow through.

Many people flake because they don't have regard for their loved ones, but a lot of the time we become flakers when we're in a hard place in life. Maybe you've had a setback on your healing journey, or you're finally practising tough self-love, and this has taken a lot out of you. Or perhaps you're going through a difficult time, and you can't bring yourself to see people because you don't want to talk about it. Maybe you don't have the energy, or you feel bad about yourself after all the self-reflection, or you're confused as to who your true friends are now that you've looked back and assessed your experiences in order to move on.

The point is, we've all had flaky friends, or even been the flake ourselves, and there are reasons for this that aren't just surface level.

I was a huge flake when I first started my healing journey at 21. The idea of seeing people when I was hurting caused me anxiety, and I was a nervous wreck the week before a plan came around that I had agreed to. As a result, I made excuses. I cancelled last minute. I promised to meet people but never followed through, with the words 'It's been so long, we must catch up!' losing their meaning over time. Some of my friends gave up on me. Others didn't stop trying. Maybe they knew that I was going through something. They thought I would eventually come around. And I did. One evening I stepped out of the house after months of persuasion to go for dinner with some work friends – who ended up being my best friends for a while – and it was the best decision I'd made in a long time.

I left the restaurant and stepped out into the dark night, lit up by streetlamps, smiling from cheek to cheek, having laughed so much that my face hurt. The moon was hanging low, a white puffy balloon, and the stars shone brightly. It was a magical evening. I was relieved. I felt lighter. Happier. I was so proud of myself for finally taking up the chance to go out and speak to friends, even if it wasn't about my problems. And this worked wonderfully. My decision to go out to see them was about showing up for them after months of flaking, but it ended up improving my night too. So, seeing my friends contributed to their happiness, but it did so much more for me because it reminded me how healing a wonderful night out with your loved ones can be for you.

> Relationships are not about give and take, but there is some level of consistency between how much you show up for others and how much they show up for you. One-sided relationships don't work, and if you feel like you're giving too much and not getting enough in return, talk to them.

If you've been a flake for a while, someone who can't seem to make the plans – then maybe it's time to reflect. And this reflection is an act of self-love, because not only will you work on why you can't be there for others, you will figure out how to be there for yourself too. So, ask yourself why you can't bring yourself to step out of the house. Why the thought of seeing others causes a ball of anxiety to form at the pit of your stomach. Why you'd rather be the 'bad friend', 'unreliable sibling' or 'selfish person' instead of showing up when you're needed. Why does the thought of showing up seem so much harder? Honest communication is the answer to it all.

This isn't just limited to you but to those that you love too. If you have a friend who's constantly backing out of plans or saying that they will meet you but not following through – then reach out to them. Talk to them. They might be going through something that you have no idea about and this regular plan-cancelling could be their cry for help. Not seeing your loved ones because of reasons out of your control can bring you down, but finding out later that they were going through something and knowing that now it's too late to help is the worst feeling in the world. I've seen people lose their loved ones due to poor mental health and the regret that clouds their face when they say the words, *'I wish I had reached out more. I thought they were busy when they kept cancelling plans and didn't reply to my messages, I wish I made more effort to be there for them, and now it's too late.'* It kills my heart.

I once heard this line in a romantic comedy called *That Awkward Moment* that went something like this: 'Being there for someone when they need you is all that relationships are.' And it's that simple. It's all you need to do. Be there for others, be there for yourself and let others be there for you.

> Instead of flaking on your people, talk to them about it, tell them what's on your mind, be honest about your lack of energy or low mood. They will understand. If they are your loved ones and a part of your safe circle, they will be there for you in spirit, even if you can't see them in person.

But meeting up with people isn't the only way of showing up for them. You show up for people in different ways, and you balance this with showing up for yourself. You give people your time, your effort, your energy, your money. You help them out when they need it. You let them turn to you on bad days and celebrate with you on good. You plan your best friend's party, your partner's holiday and your mum's retirement. You try to make it to every school assembly and sports day for your child or younger sibling. And all of this can take a huge toll on you. Sometimes it's hard to show up for everyone, and sometimes it's hard to show up for one person, even if that person is yourself.

To live a meaningful life, know when to keep saying 'yes' and when to put your foot down, no matter how difficult it is.

As you grow older, you realise how much the things that you spent so long worrying about didn't matter. It didn't matter what clothes you wore to your friend's party or whether you wished someone happy birthday at 12. It didn't matter whether you failed that test or were a few marks off a grade A. It didn't matter that everyone went shopping without you, but you were stuck babysitting at home. It didn't matter that your hair was messy when you bumped into your crush. It didn't matter when that same crush didn't like you back. It didn't matter that you lost friends along the way. As you grow older, you realise that you spent an incredible amount of time worrying about what other people thought of your appearance, your life and your goals. And when you finally 'grow up', when you finally reach that point where you're able to put on the lens of hindsight and look back at it all, you finally grasp what truly mattered. And it was never what other people thought of you — it was what you thought of yourself. What truly mattered was how patient you were, how kind you were with yourself. What mattered was how far you were willing to go to live a life that the young you would be proud of. What mattered was the amount of love and light that surrounded you. Believe me, it never mattered what others thought. It mattered what you did. It mattered what you did.

WHEN I PUT MYSELF FIRST, MY LIFE CHANGED

Earlier I mentioned that being there for my family gave me a sense of purpose and as a result, I had high regard for myself. I felt good. Useful. But often this feeling became gloomy with bitterness when things went wrong, like when my dad would plummet into alcoholism for long periods at a time.

I didn't get it. I tried so hard at being a good kid. I didn't get into trouble at school. I didn't get involved with the 'bad' crowd. I got good grades and went to university. I graduated with two degrees. I never once let my dad down. I always stood by him like a pillar when he needed me. But every time he deteriorated into alcoholism, I felt let down. I felt taken for granted. Nothing I did would ever be enough for him. I wanted to give up. It affected me so much. Of course, *it was never about me*, but because our relationships with our parents are so significant, it's nearly impossible not to be affected by their actions, even if those actions are harmful to themselves and not us directly.

Have you ever felt this way? Where you can do anything and everything for someone, but it will never change the outcome? They will always let you down, or take you for granted, or act like everything you've done for them is out of duty, or that you didn't do anything at all, and you should do more, be there for them more, show up more. Relationships like this can take a toll on you, especially if it's a relationship as close as a parent or a spouse. Because you have so many expectations from this relationship – they're supposed to be your guardian, your protector, the person that you rely on – and when they let you down, you feel like you should never have expectations from anyone ever again.

But it's in these moments that you dig into the tool bag you've been equipped with in this book and take out the tools of boundaries, honest conversations and reflective yet difficult decisions.

> *Being there for your parents is a gift. You're able to do for them what they've done for you for many years without any sense of obligation except love. But the relationships with your parents can be the most taxing. Putting your foot down in these cases is more important than any other. Putting yourself first, even if it hurts them, is okay after spending a whole lifetime of putting them first.*

There comes a point in your life where you put yourself first, no matter what. No matter how much it hurts the other person or makes them feel alone. No matter how much damage you think it's doing to your relationship at that time, believe me – putting yourself first will bring you and your relationship so much more peace in the long run. And this is perfectly aligned with balancing your relationship with others along with the relationship that you share with yourself.

The one lesson that my personal experiences have taught me, and those of you who have parents with addiction, drug misuse issues or who are toxic in their parenting will understand this: you can't pick your biological family, and you can't change them if the problems they have are too grave, but you can control how much of yourself you give them. Over the years I've developed a coping method with my dad which takes the following line of thought: be there for him when he's sober, show up when he needs you, but when he's drunk, let him go through the motions and don't get involved, unless it's serious/life-threatening.

You might not agree with me, but I hope that those who have parents with addiction will get it.

> Alcohol addiction is a medical condition with a significant mental component, meaning it can substantially alter the biology of a person's brain. If someone has alcohol addiction, their ability to stop or control their alcohol use is impaired, despite knowing the harmful consequences of continuing to abuse it.

Sure, many people with addiction will get the professional help they need and make a change in their life, *but a lot of people won't be able to*. Most people with addiction can't admit that they have a problem, no matter how many conversations you have with them. No matter how much you tell them that you're there for them through all the steps. *No matter what you do*. You could rip your chest open and give them your heart, but they still won't be able to change. My dad falls in that category. And I can't blame him. I don't know how his mind works. I don't know the ins and outs of his difficult life experiences and I will never be able to understand his pain, especially his addiction to alcohol which has lasted even longer than I've been alive.

There's no way that I can get him any help when he says he doesn't need it; unfortunately he's got a disempowering condition which alters how he sees his reality. There's nothing that I can do until he takes the first step. Every time he goes through a phase, I hear the words 'I can stop drinking, watch me,' 'I won't do it again,' and 'I was just feeling really low, but now I'm better,' until a few weeks or months of sobriety down the line and he's back in the same position.

What young me didn't understand, which I understand now, is that it's wrong to hold him accountable for his actions when, firstly, he's only partially in control of them and, secondly, they are a result of his need to cope with the trauma and hardship that he's experienced in life. His lifelong addiction has more power over him than any of us who love him can tackle. Even though he knows how damaging it is for him, he can't seem to stop. He just can't. But maybe he will one day. Maybe he will gather the strength to overpower his urges and fully practise self-love in all areas of his life, and not just some. But for now, this is as much as I get. A parent who is there most of the time but can be absent at other times. And I'm okay with it. Because when he's there he's an incredible dad. When he's there, he's all in. When he's there he's ready to go to any extent for us because he loves us, and that's more than enough for me.

I've spent my life working with him, trying to understand his addiction, urging him to forget the pain that's clawed at his chest for so many years that it's now a part of him. I've poured so much of my energy, my love and my effort into him that there came a time where I had nothing left to give except anger and resentment at why he wouldn't change. This didn't do anything for me.

So many people who have parents/relatives with addiction have told me how helpless they feel because they can't/couldn't do anything for their family member. Sometimes they can never do anything, and they're filled with regret after it's too late. I'm not going to act like I'm the first person to go through this, and I'm not the last, so I have confidence in my course of action when it comes to my dad.

journal

How would you describe your relationship with others. Is it balanced? Is there someone that you give too much of yourself to?

What is one thing you want to change in your relationship with others to help you on your self-love journey?

What one thing do you want to change in your relationship with yourself in your self-love journey?

Family can be so hard sometimes. You love them so much, but sometimes this love isn't good for you. They have the power to hurt and break you – but still, you can't help but love them. And in this dynamic, you will be picking up the broken pieces over and over again and not know what to do with them. Family can be so hard sometimes. Because you're always torn between the need to rely on them out of habit, and the desire to be your own person. And to do this you will carry out every action under the sun – you will move out, go to university, stop calling and texting them, limit your family meetings and even move country if you have to just to get the independence that you so desire. But for some reason, the emptiness will follow. The gaping hole. The piece that's missing and haunts you like a bad dream. The urge to see what they're doing and check how they are, the fear of missing out on gatherings and celebrating milestones – it will all bother you, no matter how far you go. Family can be so hard sometimes. Because you know that you should unlearn all the toxic patterns that you've taken with you and that you should stop seeking their validation. But still – every time something good happens in your life, every time you reach a new milestone, they are the first people you want to tell. Family can be so hard – because most of the time that 'well done' or 'I'm proud of you' never comes.

So, what did I do?

I stopped giving so much of myself to him. I stopped making his problems mine. I stopped feeling bad for myself when he'd throw all my hard work and help into the ocean. I admitted that he wasn't going to change, **he couldn't change**, the impact of his loss decades ago was so great that when he should have gotten the help he needed, he didn't, and now he couldn't bring himself to, and no one could force it on him. He's a grown man, there was nothing we could do other than listen to his thoughts, give him the space he needed to offload and give ourselves the space we needed away from him to clear our minds. I stopped emptying so much of myself into an imbalanced relationship where I would give and give but he wouldn't take what he needed to, nor would he have anything to give back to me. I had to put myself first. For my sanity. For myself.

The first step I took was that I stopped putting my life on hold whenever he had one of his phases. I had a habit of mourning whenever he was drinking, where I cancelled all my plans and stayed at home until he stopped. But putting my life on hold like this for days and sometimes weeks at a time wasn't good for me. I spent all my young years like this. I couldn't continue doing this into my adulthood. I was missing out on the experiences and the adventures that everyone my age was having. I was missing out on my life because my dad didn't want to live his.

The second step I took was that I no longer fought with him once he'd get sober again. Firstly, there was no point; it was like banging my head against the wall. He wouldn't be able to change, so I needed to stop expecting this. Secondly, I couldn't keep blaming him for my unhappiness. I wasn't the victim in this situation, but I made it seem like I was. He was on a healing journey that I could never understand. His pain was too raw. His heartbreak too deep. During this healing journey he had his highs as well as his lows, and the lows harmed him more than anyone else. But for so long I kept letting *his lows* become *my lows*. His actions caused me pain because *I let them*. I had to change my mindset and regain my power. My happiness lay in my hands and mine only.

The moment I started working on myself instead of trying to *fix* him – although he didn't need 'fixing', he needed to heal – my life changed for the better. I stopped giving and giving until I had nothing left. I gave him space and I gave myself space. I stopped mourning the idea of a 'perfect, sober dad' that I had created in my mind and instead appreciated the one that I got in the bright bursts of sobriety that were sprinkled throughout the years. I no longer relied on him for a sense of stability and looked to myself as the only individual who could make my life stable.

I took from this relationship what I needed to bring me joy, the moments in our life where we laughed, shared love, were there for each other and had a good time, and I refused to accept what I didn't need: the darkness, the alcohol, the pain, anger and resentment.

> Be there for others. Sure. But don't bend
> yourself backwards to make them happy.
> Don't beat yourself up about not being able to
> save them. Don't give too much of yourself
> away that you have nothing left within to give
> to yourself.

If you have someone in your life who takes and takes and doesn't give anything in return – please put yourself first. Even if the balance tips in your favour. Even if it causes feelings of guilt in the beginning. Even if it hurts you to leave them behind or let them deal with their own problems. Put yourself first. Giving so much of yourself to others won't do you any good. And this will help your relationship in the long run. You will no longer feel spiteful because they don't appreciate you or because you give too much of yourself to them. Instead, there will be cohesion. There will be balance. You will enjoy your relationship with them and take from it what serves you and throw away what doesn't.

Today, I have a tender, warm relationship with my dad. I love him and I will always worry about him, it's something I can't stop doing. But I no longer treat him like a child. I don't take the carer role when it comes to him. Instead, I treat him as an equal when I need to, and I let him treat me as his child when he wants to. He is someone who I can't live without and will turn to at every corner, but at the same time he is someone that I also need time away from to maintain a sense of peace and tranquillity, especially when he's going through a dip in his healing. This space from him is essential because it gives me strength and that allows me to be there for him *when I can do something for him*, rather than beat myself up about the things I don't have the power to change.

This shift in balance in our relationship has allowed me to make the most of my time with him, to take comfort in his presence and his love, and to prevent myself from feeling helpless, then turning bitter when he's in a difficult place in his life.

Sure, we have a duty to be there for our loved ones, and having good relationships – especially with our immediate family – is essential to living a happy and healthful life. But you're better able to be there for others when you're in a good place yourself, and if you keep letting yourself be dragged into other people's darkness, you won't be able to help them or yourself.

Whenever I'm on an aeroplane, I hear 'Put on your own oxygen mask before you help someone with theirs,' and that's how to see relationships that are imbalanced. Help yourself, and then perhaps you might be able to help your loved ones, even from a distance.

How much do you give of yourself to others? E.g., too much, not enough, a little bit, just right. How does this make you feel?

What does a balanced relationship with others look like to you?

In an ideal world, how would you like to practise self-love along with the love that you hold for others?

chapter 8

everyday challenges and social media

Practising self-love can be hard in today's world. Social media has turned the idea of self-love into something that's too picture-perfect, where you're encouraged to believe that you should be in a state of constant joy, self-satisfaction and self-appreciation – which isn't right. Alongside this, social media has consumed so much of our lives that, to begin with, we need to consider: what kind of world is it that we're walking on the path to self-love in?

This is a world heavily dominated by social media apps where '*socialising*' means liking and commenting on each other's photos and sending each other memes, and spending 'quality time' with your family/friends means WhatsApping, FaceTiming or calling them. A world where your social life is ranked by how exciting your online profile looks, and how popular you are is decided by the number of followers you have.

This is a world where social media apps are downloaded in the blink of an eye, a world where you check in on your favourite influencers more than you do your loved ones. A world where you log into social media for useful life tips and advice, such as visiting an influencer's profile to figure out whether a skincare product is good, rather than running it by an expert or researching its ingredients. A world where your belief of what makes for a *great life* is heavily influenced by the content that you consume online. This is the world in which you do the difficult work, the world in which you have the cutting conversations with your former self, where you dive deep, and rewind, and reconsider who you are and what to do to love yourself and make progress in your healing.

In this world, you're forced to compare your physical appearance, your life, your happiness, your job, your family and everything else to other people's. In this world, loving yourself becomes a journey that challenges you at every edge and corner. So, what do you do? You face these challenges, and you conquer your fears.

Roughly how many hours a day do you spend on social media?

Would you like to lower this, or are you happy with your consumption?

We've become so used to putting on a show for everyone that sometimes we forget that after the curtains close, when we are by ourselves, all alone, in the comforting silence of our own presence, that we can be ourselves now. Why have we become this way? Why do we think that it's easier to lock away our innermost scariest thoughts rather than face them, rather than gather the courage to deal with them? Why have we become a generation walking on eggshells around each other and refusing to say anything that might offend someone to such an extent that we don't even have the strength to offend ourselves? Because all I see going forward is a generation filled with people with so many unresolved issues, so much to say and do, and no willpower to go through with it. And no courage to face any of our battles. And no faith in ourselves. And no belief that we are our biggest strength, not our biggest weakness.

How Technology Has Changed Our Lives

Think about your day-to-day life. What's the first thing that you do after you wake up? A day in your life might look like this: you make your bed and brush your teeth, after which you cook a delicious breakfast, or get breakfast on the go, jump in the car/train/bus, grab a piping hot drink from the café closest to your workplace and head into the office for a day of work. The rest of your day is divided in unequal chapters of replying to emails, answering calls, filling out spreadsheets, catching up with your workmates and taking generous tea/coffee breaks, all while the clock at the back of your head is slowly tick-tocking towards 5pm, or the end of your shift.

But wait, we forgot the most important component of your day: the mindless scrolling that you do on your phone every time that you're bored.

The average Joe checks his phone right after he wakes up. After that, he brushes his teeth, gets ready and heads off to work. But before heading off to work, he sits down to have breakfast, his phone in his left hand and a piece of toast in his right, and he swipes, likes and takes a bite until the plate is empty but his brain is full of all the fruitless content he's just consumed. Then he gets into his car and drives to work, but if he gets on the train or the bus then the phone is back in his right hand and the scrolling, swipes and likes continue until the journey to work ends.

Our days are a blur of emails, phone calls, lots of caffeine, chitchat and <u>endless social media consumption</u>.

Joe checks his phone the moment it vibrates, disturbing his workflow. He scrolls through TikTok when he's taking a five-minute break from the computer screen. He takes his phone with him to his ten-minute hot drink breaks, making coffee with his right hand and swiping with his left. Heck, Joe even takes his phone to the toilet, because *God forbid* if he were to miss an important reel, and he doesn't want to be bored in the toilet – or worse, be left alone with his thoughts!

This routine is okay in the grand scheme of things. 'It's not that deep, Ruby,' you might say. What else are you supposed to kill time with on your lunch and tea breaks? Well, a book, maybe? Or an educational podcast?

Okay, fine, I admit that I'm no better in this department and have become victim to the social media hype too. *So who am I to judge?* It's okay to use gadgets. I mean, we live in a world where people seem to buy new gadgets almost as often as they buy new clothes, so we can't expect to not be drawn to them. In fact, our smartphones – and the social media apps within them – have been *designed to draw us in*, with thousands of engineers working to create the kind of systems that constantly peel our attention away from the real world and focus it on the *reel* one.

Technology itself is not the concern; in fact, it's a great innovation in our advancing culture. The concern is the way that we let it affect our daily lives. Technology has become a funhouse mirror that reflects and magnifies all our insecurities back at us. We let it strip away our confidence because of the dissimilarities between us and others who appear better than us. We engage in comparison, in rejection of our own realities, in idolising social media constructs that do nothing for us. The way that you consume social media can become a threat to your self-love journey. That's why it's important to use technology in the right way. Yes, technology *can* be good, but you must learn how to harvest its benefits like the modern-day farmers that I know you are.

What does a normal day in your life look like?

Do you make your bed, brush your teeth and get ready for work in that order, or is your phone a constant component in all three of those activities and more?

Try and be more mindful when you wake up tomorrow. Try not to pick up your phone first thing in the morning. If you want to use it on the way to work, use it to listen to a podcast or read a book.

See how long you can get through your morning without logging into social media.

The Social Media Problem

The amount of time that we spend on our phones wouldn't be a waste if we were doing it to read a health and positivity journal, to watch an insightful documentary, to listen to a self-improvement podcast or to learn new skills. Instead, we mind-numbingly hop from one social media app to the other and either entertain ourselves through silly, humorous TikToks and memes, or devour the highlight reels of other people's lives before a feeling of apprehension overwhelms us and we decide to put our phone aside.

The problem is that when we put our phone away, we return to our own *mediocre* life where we're currently sat in front of a computer screen, entering numbers on a spreadsheet in our mind-numbing 9–5 or maybe we enjoyed our 9–5 up until the moment we opened our phone and saw someone else's life that looked better than ours.

How would you feel returning to your spreadsheet after you've seen a vlog of an influencer on a life-changing South African safari? How would you feel in the dull grey open-plan office that you work in after coming across a 'day in the life' of someone displaying their pristine work-from-home setup?

Yep, not great.

> Comparison is the biggest threat to living a
> happy and fulfilled life.

Consider Joe. Joe compares himself daily to Jay, the athlete with an eight-pack whom Joe has been following on Instagram for years now. Joe hates his love handles, and he's guilty of not stepping foot in the gym in the last two months, with his membership another expense piercing a hole in his pocket. What makes him feel worse is when Jay posts a video of himself shirtless and lifts his shorts up to reveal his incredible quads and calves.

Joe wonders how it's possible for anyone to look this good.

It isn't possible.

With the introduction of social media apps came innumerable filters and beauty apps that allow you to add abs, slim down your waist, make your eyes bigger, thicken your bum/cheeks/hair and turn yourself into an Instagram model if you want. These apps thrive by feeding off people's insecurities.

If Jay had a good day in the gym but still couldn't see his abs as clearly as he hoped, all he'd have to do is go on an app like AirBrush and add them in. As a result, when Joe comes across Jay's photo, he believes that Jay is working hard in the gym (which he is) and *that's* why he looks so great. *That would also explain why Jay gets all the girls*. Joe would mentally berate himself, telling himself that he doesn't get girls like Jay does because he doesn't have abs. After seeing the photo Jay posted, Joe might spend the remainder of the day feeling bad about himself, as though he doesn't already have enough on his plate.

But let's assume for the sake of argument that Jay *does* really have an eight-pack (which isn't physically possible to retain for long without starving yourself or taking steroids, but anyway), and he works hard for it.

Why does Joe still feel so bad?

Well, there might be many reasons for this, such as low self-worth, childhood trauma, insecurities and fears, but the crux of it lies in the use of social media itself.

If everywhere you look people seem to be doing better than you, it's very hard not to think that there's something wrong with you. It's

*very hard to love yourself, especially when
you're going through a hard time.*

Social media has a damaging effect on self-esteem and self-confidence. Everywhere you look online, you see people who are better looking, more successful and living more complete lives that make yours look bleak in comparison; this makes it very hard to have positive thoughts about yourself. It's very hard not to talk down to yourself or feel anger at not being able to achieve the same things as your high school friends who are on six-figure incomes, soon to be married and start a family, or are on a life-changing trip around the world. And it's especially hard when you're going through a difficult time in your life.

journal

*When was the last time you had a negative thought about
your appearance, house, material items, family,
achievements, etc., after logging online?*

*Can you see a correlation between your negative feelings
and accessing social media?*

HIGHLIGHT REELS CAN BE OUR WORST NIGHTMARE

When viewing the 'highlight reel' of other people's lives – the positive, most beautiful parts that they share on social media – we're in a perpetually anxious state. The perfection that we see online results in a sense of increased pressure: we think that we should also look that good, have that much money, go on as many holidays as that person does, have a big house and a shiny car and the perfect family. But nothing on social media is a true reflection of the whole picture. People are often quick to filter out the bad parts of their day and only share the good, and although this might appear harmless, this inaccurate picture can be damaging for those whose insecurities are triggered when they come across these filtered highlights online.

That is just what social media does – it supplies various opportunities for our insecurities and fears to be triggered.

When you open Instagram and Kiran from high school has shared a cheery photo of her, her husband and their three-month-old baby in a sunny resort in Barbados, you instantly think that Kiran has it all: the ideal man, a beautiful baby and the perfect balance in her life. But here's the truth: Kiran didn't post the 2am feeds, the sleepless nights and the bouts of low mood that overwhelmed her in her postnatal days. Kiran didn't post the argument that she had with her husband only minutes ago over who will wake up with the baby during the night.

Even though Kiran doesn't live the picture-perfect life that she shows on social media, because life *isn't perfect* and nothing is ever sunshine and roses, this does nothing to stop the tangy mist of envy that's formed at the pit of your stomach when you come across this photo. We're not stupid; we know deep down that people only show their best bits, but it's hard not to compare our failures with other people's successes and our insecurities with what we perceive as their perfection. This causes a negatively charged narrative to form in our mind, one that's condescending. Harsh words such as 'You will never be happy,' 'You're such a failure,' or subtler ones such as 'This person has so much going for them, I wish I did too,' and 'Will I ever be as successful/pretty/rich as them?' thump in your mind whenever you come across other people's highlight reels.

This is even more the case when you're in a difficult place, such as on a healing journey that takes a lot out of you.

I HAVE FOMO

The number of times that I've logged onto social media, having enjoyed my day, and suddenly felt bad after seeing someone's fancy day out with their friends, or story highlights of their holiday, *is unbelievable*. And that's just what social media does. It sets unrealistic expectations for you of what your life, achievements and relationships should look like, and you run with that standard in mind as opposed to what would truly make you happy.

> *When we see other people enjoying themselves online, we develop a fear that we're wasting our lives by not living fully like they are.*

I like to believe that I'm a homebody. My ideal date night with Ivnit is cuddling up under a blanket and watching a Marvel movie while we enjoy our favourite food: Nepalese momos (dumplings), spicy chicken chow mein and sweet masala chai (tea, folks, tea). Weird combo, I know. But my love bucket is full after those dates. I'm happy. Content. Loved.

But I wasn't always convinced of what made me happy in my relationship.

In the past, when I logged onto social media and saw a couple out on a date in their glamorous clothes, eating at a fancy restaurant and having a great time, *I would want it too*. I'd quickly make a reservation at a restaurant for the following week. I'd wear my best dress, the most glamorous and the most uncomfortable too, pair it with some high heels and slap on lots of makeup (I hate putting on makeup) and head into London with my beau. Would I have a good time? Of course I would. I love spending time with my partner. But would I have been more comfortable and *enjoyed myself more* if I was chilling in my PJs with Marvel, my man and some Nepalese takeaway? Hell yes! I would swap any glamorous date for my homely, chill ones. But it took me a while to figure this out.

Social media encourages this *FOMO* culture, where we see other people's lives and think that we're not living life to the same extent that they are. So, we follow them. We make a reservation at the restaurant they went to; we book the same hotel for our next holiday; we go on the same adventures and do what they did rather than what we would have wanted to. And we're never truly satisfied. The food is too bland, the hotel not as nice as it looked online – the entire trip a glamorous image created only for the eyes of social media.

Deep down we know that social media isn't real, and other people's online profiles aren't a true reflection of their life. But they look happy. They look *great*, in fact. And we believe that we will be just as happy as they are if we do what they're doing. This is especially the case when we're feeling down and under and we see someone looking as sunny as we would like to feel.

Until we no longer feel this fear of missing out when we go online, as well as this constant need to compare, we will continue to be dissatisfied with lives that we're actually quite content in living.

When was the last time you saw a social media post and instantly bought the clothing, makeup or homewares being displayed, or booked the holiday, restaurant or activity that was posted about?

Was it as good as it looked online?

I GOT SO MANY LIKES ON THIS PHOTO!

Social media has also resulted in our seeking validation from others, and this is disadvantageous for anyone on a self-love journey. Social media is an easy way to seek instant gratification: you take a photo, slap a filter on it and share it online with a few catchy hashtags. As the number of likes increases, so does your mood. You even smile when some of your friends compliment you in the comments, and suddenly you feel better about yourself.

The problem with this is that the number of likes starts to affect how you see yourself: fewer likes equates to a 'bad photo' and no comments means that there's something wrong with you.

You might have felt great about yourself before you posted that picture, but now that you see the lack of enthusiasm from your followers/online friends, you don't like the photo – or even yourself – anymore. But where did your self-validation go? Where did your own enthusiasm about the photo go?

Apps like Instagram that were introduced to connect us with our family and friends are now a means of validation, where we look to get as many likes and comments as possible to get that high of the day. Apps like TikTok fed on this desire and have become exceptionally popular in a short period; going 'viral' and catching the attention of millions of people supplies all those seeking validation through social media with the high that they need. But this is extremely harmful to our self-confidence. We're relying on likes, comments and views to determine whether a piece of content we initially enjoyed creating is valuable or not. We're then extending how we feel about the response to our online content to how we feel about ourselves.

Apps like Instagram have tried to deal with this by giving the option to hide the like count of photos. This was a great idea. But although it worked in the beginning in dealing with the 'likes and self-confidence problem', it didn't really help in the long run. As time went on, creators began hiding the like count of posts that didn't do as well as they hoped while showing the like count on the posts that had great engagement. I myself fell victim to this, and even though I've tried for years to not let the likes and engagement of my online posts get to me, it still does.

I can understand content creators by pointing out that they need decent engagement in the form of likes and comments to get paid well from the brands that they work with, as social media is their bread and butter, and the primary way to decide whether someone's page is doing well is through their engagement. But when the need for online engagement bleeds into your view of yourself, that's when you need to worry.

That's why it's important to look at the ways in which social media can negatively hinder your healing journey, and your path to self-love and manifesting happiness, before finding a solution to this problem. Because we can't get rid of social media, and walking on your self-love path is so important, so we need to find a way that we can make both things work.

> Social media is often seen as a power for evil, causing disconnection, social isolation and alienating its users, but it's also a power for good, feeding knowledge, allowing connection and breeding confidence — if we use it the right way.

exercise

Look back at your week and note down the number of times you've found yourself comparing yourself to a stranger online.

Is there a pattern between the kind of pages you follow online and how you feel about yourself?

Try to actively limit how much access you have to the content that makes you feel bad about yourself for the next month. If you see something that causes a twitch in your gut, swipe past it instantly or unfollow that page.

Register how you're feeling at the end of each week. This activity should make you feel better about yourself in the long run.

Go easy on yourself. Stop scrolling on your phone, a frown padding your forehead as you compare yourself to the highlight reels of others, and instead take a deep breath. Remind yourself who you are, where you've come from and just how testing the journey itself was. Be tender with your heart — it has seen too much in the short span of life that you've lived and it needs to be cherished. It needs to be taken care of. It needs to be shared only with those who will know how to be gentle with it. Go easy on yourself. Don't think about your past mistakes or regrets, or the people you've left behind, and instead focus on the present. Focus on the love you currently have in your life and the people who would go to the ends of the earth for you. Forget about who was and think about who is standing beside you. Treat yourself with warmth, with patience, with care — the same way that you would treat someone that you love — and remind yourself of how far you've come. Of how strong you are. Go easy on yourself. Stop running after people, things or dreams and just slow down. If something hasn't worked out yet, then just be patient. What is yours will come to you. What is yours will come to you.

Social Media and Your Healing Journey

Social media consumption is already harmful to the average person's self-esteem, but if you consider someone who has just lost their job, had their heart broken, someone who doesn't have money, or someone who is struggling with their body image, then the influence of social media is truly worrying. Because if you just lost your job and you see a photo of your childhood friend's recent promotion, then you will feel worse about your situation. If you came across a photo of someone showing off their perfect swimsuit body after comfort eating a tub of Ben & Jerry's, you might start to feel guilty and even dislike yourself. If you just had your heart broken and came across a post about true love, then – if you're like me – you might want to smash your phone against a wall in frustration.

Because heartbreak sucks. So does losing your job, having an eating disorder, experiencing a close one's death, feeling anxiety, low mood, failure or facing any difficult obstacle in your life. But it sucks even more when you try to escape your pain by logging into social media only to be reminded how alone you are in feeling that pain.

*Social media can be very isolating because
when you log online, it can seem as though
everyone is living and moving on except you.
It can seem as though everyone is happy
except you.*

Imagine that you've been healing from a broken marriage for the last six months. You're fighting the monsters in your head, you've created a safe space with your support circle, you engage in self-care activities in the form of morning runs and weekly Pilates classes and you've even started group therapy. Then you come across Kiran's photo on Instagram. You see her glowing face. You notice the way her husband has placed his hand on her shoulder and the adorable infant that they hold between them, and suddenly there's a sharp knife piercing through your chest. You no longer feel okay.

Until that moment, you were having a great Sunday. You enjoyed a productive morning and finished all your chores. You took your dog out for a walk and got some much-needed sunshine. You spent the afternoon listening to a popular health podcast, with today's episode conveniently on heartbreak, while completing an at-home gym workout. You caught up with your mum over the phone and you felt good. Better than good. You were doing well. But when you saw Kiran's photo, all the raw memories of your broken marriage came rushing back.

Kiran and her husband look so happy, and suddenly you feel like a failure. You start participating in negative self-talk. You think about your insecurities, your mistakes, your weaknesses. You think about your flaws. You start forming damaging beliefs about yourself. The unforgiving voice in your head tells you that there was something wrong with you and that's why it didn't work out. You replay the breakdown of your relationship in your mind on repeat, and you forget to breathe.

The thing is, until that moment in your day – you were fine. It was one of your better days, and you were making progress in moving on. You took part in several self-care activities, you even exercised tough self-love when you took out your wedding dress to give to charity. But seeing the highlight reel of Kiran's life triggered you in many ways, and the mental comparison that you took part in overwhelmed you.

This is one way in which social media consumption can have a negative effect on your self-love journey. Because you're doing the hard work. You're practising both easy and tough self-love. You're establishing your boundaries and expectations and still, *still*, when you log online you find yourself in the same place all over again. This causes you to form destructive narratives in your mind that say you're still standing in one place. You're walking but not moving at all.

exercise

Your smartphone has a setting which allows you to set a bedtime on your phone, at which point it goes into 'do not disturb' mode. Even the background lighting changes, allowing you to adjust to the darkness in your room and motivating you to put your phone away and go to sleep.

Set this up for a specific bedtime every day and put your phone away when you're urged to.

My bedtime mode starts at 10.30pm and ends at 7am. As someone who had a terrible sleeping pattern, this setting has been an absolute life changer!

Remember: *it takes approximately 21 days for an action to become a habit, so, even if it's hard in the beginning, don't give up!*

I've struggled with my body image my entire life because of the emotional abuse I experienced when I was a tubby child, so I know how it feels to engage in regular toxic comparison. I still engage in regular self-criticism without realising it, picking at my lower belly and muttering 'I look so fat' under my breath until someone points it out, and I stop abruptly. The thing is, I don't want to engage in self-criticism, but it's something I've done for so long that I don't even realise when I'm doing it. It's a learning curve, something that I will always struggle with. It's one of the self-love tasks that will be at the top of my list forever.

Consider someone recovering from an eating disorder. They have always had body image issues and they want to move on from this, and now they are walking on the path to self-love. Social media has the potential to be their biggest obstacle, because one of the biggest forms of comparison we take part in when we're scrolling online is how we look in relation to others.

> Research has found that most women and many men engage in negative comparison of their body to others when they log online, and this is very injurious to the love they hold for themselves.

The 'ideal body' is a myth, but the way that this ideal has been portrayed in society, the media and now social media has affected millions of people over the years – I'm talking thousands of years of history. In fact, if we look at just the last hundred years, we can see how the ideal body shape for a woman has gone from a cinched waist and hourglass figure, to a slender, curvaceous body, to big breasts and large hips, to an extremely thin figure, to a toned, slim body, and now back to the hourglass figure with thick thighs and God knows what else.

People have a lot to say about the ideal body, specifically the ideal woman's body. This dialogue has always existed, but never has this dialogue had the power to affect as many people around the world as it does now. Because we have technology. Because we have social media.

This form of comparison is already so injurious that people's self-perception can be dented forever, and it can result in embarrassment, shame and low mood in people of many ages. Even children who are just starting to develop a sense of self have been reported to point out that they have physical flaws. I've seen little girls as young as six pointing out that they will gain weight if they eat too much. This is ridiculous to me, but as someone who was told she was over-weight aged seven, I'm not surprised.

If you're exposed to certain body types on social media, specific-ally men and women with the *'ideal body'*, then you're likely to experience body shame.

> Body shaming is when someone criticises or mocks the shape and size of your body. We can feel body shame as well, fostering harmful beliefs about the way that we look to ourselves and others when we have low self-esteem.

I comfort ate a lot when I first started my healing journey at 21, and when I logged online and saw girls who looked slimmer and better than me, I felt terrible about myself. It made forming posi-tive narratives about who I was and what I deserved very difficult, and this is so important when you're trying to make progress in your healing. And social media can do this. Social media can tarnish your sense of self and send you plunging into a well of insecurities.

> Social media can be the saint and the sinner. At the end of the day, it depends on how you let it move you.

But is social media truly the enemy? I'm afraid not. We can blame social media as much as we want for the negative beliefs we foster, but social media isn't our real enemy. The way that we use it is. If you use it correctly, social media has the power to be your saviour. But to understand how, we first need to look at why things have gotten this bad.

Why have we let technology and social media apps consume us entirely?

One by one open the top three social media apps you use and check your 'following' lists.

How many friends are you following?

How many of these are inspirational pages?

How many of these are memes?

Go through your 'following' list and do a cleanse:

✳   *Unfollow accounts that you don't engage with.*

✳   *Unfollow accounts that bring you negativity, e.g., body image issues, jealousy, comparison, etc.*

✳   *Unfollow accounts of people you no longer talk to.*

✳   *Unfollow accounts that you follow for the sake of keeping up with someone's life who adds no value to yours.*

In this digital age, social media comparison can weigh heavy on us. Constantly logging in to find other people living 'their best lives' can take a toll on your self-esteem, decrease your confidence and lessen the amount of love you hold for yourself. The need to be as picture-perfect as those we see online, the desire to have our lives figured out in the way that they have, the anxiousness when we think about how little we've done, achieved or experienced according to the highlight reels that others present all negatively affect our happiness. The way to deal with this constant comparison culture is to remind yourself how far you have come in your own journey — and no one else's. There are so many hurdles you've crossed over the years. Battles you've both won and lost. People who left you behind or those you had to leave in order to move on. Regrets that turned into tools for growth and change. You should be incredibly proud of how much you've achieved. Not in terms of material possessions but in terms of wisdom. In terms of experiences. In terms of love and friendship. In terms of mental and emotional growth. And I understand that sometimes logging online or seeing people around you can be overwhelming — but it's in those moments of anxiety and fear that you remember who you were, who you've become and how much further you are yet to go in your journey.

Social Media Is Not the Enemy

The biggest issue is that we've forgotten why these apps existed in the first place. Social media apps were a way of revolutionising the connections that we had with the people around us and extending our reach further, across the country and even the world, where we could create contacts, network and build relationships with people everywhere. Relationships that – if nourishing – could be ground-breaking in your healing journey.

But we no longer use our online apps just to connect; instead, we use them to escape from our problems – only to find reasons to have more.

Many times, we spend hours on social media without having connected with any of our friends and family, instead scrolling through memes, photos and reels from random strangers who add nothing to our lives. The purpose of social media was to bring us closer, but for some reason it's pushing us further away from our loved ones, and we can't solely blame an app for this when we're in charge of how we use it. We're the masters of our minds, after all.

In the beginning of our relationship, after a long day's work I'd find myself pointing out to Ivnit that he didn't drop me a message all day, and that our phone conversation in the morning had been our only one. His reply was, 'Yes, but I was thinking about you during my lunch break. Didn't you see all the memes I sent you?' Ivnit believed that he'd communicated with me because he sent me memes. Firstly, *men, I tell you*. Secondly, after receiving this response a few times, I explained to him that sending memes on social media is different from picking up the phone or dropping someone a message.

I know what you're thinking: shouldn't I have addressed my own attachment issues because one phone conversation in the morning was not enough for me? And I did address this, I promise.

Relationships are a work in progress, but the point I'm making is that so many people see social media contact, like sending memes, as a normal form of communication, and when you log online you feel even more disconnected from those that you love, especially if you're in a bad place.

Suppose that you and Kiran are best friends, but she hasn't messaged you since she went on holiday. This is understandable, except Kiran knows that you're going through a challenging time in your life, and when you come across her photo you might believe that she's moving on without you, with her husband and her child. You feel unseen, or worse, neglected by her.

But if you picked up your phone and saw a message from Kiran, one that either reminded you that she was thinking of you, or one that was honest about how her holiday is going (contrary to the highlight), then you would feel better. You might not even feel the knife stabbing in your chest when you see the photo because you would know the whole picture. It's not that knowing the whole picture will make you feel better about yourself, but that knowing the whole picture will serve as a reminder that everyone has their ups and downs.

As a result, Kiran's photo might prompt you to celebrate the highlights of your journey too, such as the Sunday you just had. Knowing the whole picture will serve as a token that the photo Kiran posted was a highlight of her life, but not her entire life summarised, and this is the case with all our highlight reels.

One way to counteract the anxiousness that you feel when you open your social media app is to use it to communicate with your loved ones through messaging and contacting them. Social media is exceptional in its ability to connect you with people everywhere, and it's a blessing to be able to contact your best friend even when she's thousands of miles away on holiday.

Use social media to build your connections with the people that you love, rather than to see the brightest parts of their lives without any background information on what they might be experiencing. Because not only will viewing highlights cause a disconnection between you and them (because of the narrative that *'I'm unhappy and she's having a great time without me'*), but it will also push you to build false beliefs about their life and their experiences. This will create distance between you and your loved ones, and that's not something you need when you're walking on your path to self-love and creating a happy, comfortable life for yourself.

exercise

All smartphones have a setting via which you can see your phone usage, with detailed information on which apps are being used the most, and what hours during the day you are most active on your phone. Go to your smartphone's settings now and find the data on how many hours a day you spend looking at your phone (on my phone this is the 'Digital Wellbeing' setting and on iPhones it's called 'Screen Time').

If you're unable to find this setting, there are plenty of digital health apps that you can download via the app store. It's a great idea to research the best ones before you download one.

Once you have them, the stats should show you how much time during the day you're spending on social media. Ideally, you don't want to spend more than two hours a day accessing anything on your phone.

Your smartphone has a setting which allows you to put a daily time limit on certain apps. This means that after the number of hours are met, you can no longer access those apps until the next day.

If you're over the recommended two hours of usage, set yourself a limit of four hours a day to use your phone to start with, and after the first week reduce this to two hours a day. After another week try reducing it further, to one hour a day.

Once you've done this, ask yourself: how do you feel now? Do you miss your phone time, or have you found other things to fill those moments in your life when you used to reach for social media?

Loving myself has never been easy. I struggle with it to this day and I don't know why. In a world where we constantly talk about 'self-love', 'self-worth' and how to be the best version of yourself, I fail to grasp what the best version of me looks like. Is she kind and soft-hearted, or is she loud, boisterous and unapologetic? Does she take herself on walks, dates and to the movies alone, or does she rely on her loved ones for companionship and happiness? Does the best version of me enjoy red-hot, bitter lattes or sweet ones, swirled with caramel syrup and ice cubes? Because I've sailed through the various hues of pain, pleasure and healing and have found a different 'me' each time. And in a world where we keep telling ourselves that we're worthy, I find myself wondering which one of those 'me's' is worthy. The one that dived through heartache and curled up in a ball in a corner of her room, or the one who woke up in the morning and gave herself another chance? The one who let go of people who broke her or the one who loved, unabashedly, without a care for the consequences that would ensue? Because loving yourself shouldn't be this hard. It shouldn't be such a challenge. And maybe I'm overthinking. Maybe everyone knows just who they are and has figured it all out, or maybe, just maybe — others have realised that loving yourself doesn't mean knowing yourself entirely. Instead, it means giving yourself room to grow and evolve. Loving yourself means accepting who you are, as imperfect as you are today, without worrying about who you might become.

The Social Media Solution

In the beginning of my healing journey, logging online was equivalent to tossing myself back in the gloomy pit of misery. I spent entire evenings huddled up on my bed with tears streaming down my face before escaping my thoughts by going online. I'd log on and instead of finding an escape, I found couples who were in love, friends who were on holiday, families out at dinners, my old friends getting new jobs or promotions and practically everyone that I knew moving on joyfully in their lives. They all looked so happy. Happier than me.

Logging online was like getting slapped across the face. Each photo was a reminder of how little I had and how much of a failure I was in every aspect. I'd continue to scroll through the photos, observing the lightest moments of other people's lives and feeling intense pity for myself. Social media served as a reminder that I was unhappy, unloved and unprotected because I had no safe space to return to. Logging online in my darkest times showed me all that I had lost and how hard my life was.

But this is where I was mistaken, because I didn't understand the power of social media to change my reality for good, not for bad.

I USED SOCIAL MEDIA TO SAVE MYSELF

I was doing what we all do – comparing the beginning of my mountain trek to someone who had reached the peak in theirs. But here's the magic of it all: going online did more to save me than anything else could.

Instagram had it all, so I started searching for stuff that might help me, particularly for healing and self-love quotes, quotes about mental health, heartbreak and moving on, videos about letting go. And the results were astounding. This is where I discovered some of my favourite online poets, particularly R.M. Drake and Najwa Zebian, and I was saved.

So much of what I read online resonated with me. I felt heard and listened to. I felt understood. I decided to buy their books and then buy books by other authors whose work was similar. Over time I discovered some incredible self-love authors such as Bianca Sparacino, Brianna Weist and others.

Through reading books and online posts, I noticed that I was slowly getting better. With each piece that I came across, I found a layer of my heart threading itself back together. The mornings felt lighter, the evenings calmer. I spent an hour each evening scrolling through poetry and healing pages, pages dedicated to mental health, pages run by therapists, doctors and writers who wanted to help others through their content. The more that I searched, the more I found the answers that I was looking for. This was my therapy.

I also discovered that there were countless online communities with people like me who were having a hard time and were looking for an escape online, people who felt listened to through the content they accessed, people who were connecting and building relationships with others and finding themselves all over again. People who were healing along the way.

At some point, I also began sharing my words online and building a community. I started healing and using my words to heal others.

Books had always been a means of escape for me. I stumbled across my first second-hand bookstore in one of the weekend markets where my dad worked. My dad and his brothers would set up a market stall on the weekends and sell new and second-hand mobile phones, colour-changing lights, fibre optic lamps, car stereos and audio equipment, radios, frames, and so much more. While kids my age went to the park or the beach with their family, I'd happily wake up at 4.30am on a Saturday and Sunday to go to work with my dad.

I remember that day very clearly: I was on a mission to buy some hot dogs and tea, loose change jingling in my back pocket as I skipped blissfully past rows and rows of stalls, the faint burr of chatter all around; and suddenly, I stopped short, my breath catching in my throat as I noticed a makeshift bookshop tucked away in the corner of a long line of stalls. Before I knew it, I found myself gliding scrawny fingers over dog-eared second-hand books with fluorescent covers, the bold font titles luring me in. I had no idea that this moment would change my life forever.

I always wanted to be an author, and I had a plan too. I'd do a teacher training degree and give myself a year after that to write a novel and submit it to agents. But social media changed it all around for me. The online resources I accessed as I was healing gave me the bright idea to share my writing there too. I had so much within me to share, about love, heartbreak, healing. About mental health and moving on. The words streamed out of me and onto the digital page that I'd post, my fist in my mouth as I anxiously waited for the results.

The outcome of putting my faith in social media was me ending up with an online community of nearly a million people, five self-published books and the good fortune to write this very special book and publish it with my dream publishing company. I've had so many opportunities through trusting social media, opportunities that young me would never have dreamed of.

Social media changed my life forever. It fast-tracked my career, allowed me to realise my dreams and helped me on my road to recovery

*from my past trauma through giving me
access to a community of like-minded people
who wanted to heal alongside me.*

What I've learned from my experiences is this: at this point in history, you have more tools and resources available to you than any other generation. Resources that can educate you, enlighten you and save you. You just need make use of them. You just need to use social media in a way that will benefit you. This is quite an intuitive process and must be grounded in the desire to heal yourself, especially in today's day and age. When I was healing from a hard heartbreak, Instagram was the major platform, and that's what I used to help myself. There was no TikTok, no reels, no shorts. There were not as many videos on how to heal from heartbreak, how to improve your confidence, how to move on. No inspiring quotes with resounding background music that could change your mood instantly and motivate you. No instant access to life-changing information in the form of 60-second videos from doctors, spiritual leaders, motivational speakers, healers. It's brilliant, how far we've come.

And you have access to all of it, and more. You don't just have one social media app at your disposal but countless apps that are created to engage you, heal you and motivate you, apps that teach you life tips, give you the ultimate hacks, apps designed to provide content that inspires you, that encourages you to do better, to be better.

But of course, sometimes it can be consuming, especially with the amount of content at your disposal. It's okay to feel overwhelmed or not use every available resource. It's okay to take it easy. The point isn't that you should storm through your healing by using all the online tools available to you, the point is to become aware that social media is not your enemy. When you're drowning in self-neglect after watching a video about someone's fitness journey, just know that you can swipe down and find something that can help you. Or you can switch it off entirely. It's completely up to you.

I always talk about the self-care influencers who go on 5am morning runs, but I'm genuinely inspired by them. Waking up and switching my phone on to find someone living their best life encourages me to live mine. It's no longer a reminder of my own inadequacy but a token of strength and inspiration. If someone else can put this much effort into improving their life, then what's to stop me?

> Use the content you see online to be inspired
> and encouraged to live your best life. Other
> people excelling and doing well should remind
> you that you can do it too.

If you're learning to love yourself and are an avid user of social media apps, then instead of using them to escape your life and, as a result, feel bad about yourself, aim to use them to your advantage. Find *helpful* online resources. Search for pages that give you advice and support, pages that help you get what you're looking for.

journal

Are you inspired by any people online? Who are they?

*What's your favourite travel page, lifestyle page,
motivational quotes page?*

Do you log online when you want a recipe for something?

Have you ever seen a post or video that moved you and changed the weather of your mood?

For example, if you want to start writing a journal but are unsure how to begin, look for journalling apps or follow journalling accounts on Instagram or TikTok to learn more about it. If seeing dog photos calms you down, follow lots of cute dog pages. If you feel better after reading a daily affirmation, download a mindfulness app or follow a mindfulness account and turn on your notifications. If you want to start meditating, or practising yoga, or even learning how to cook, log into your social media. The depth and breadth of information on social media is astounding. There are so many talented individuals who create magnificent and engaging content. Whether it's cooking, cleaning, engineering, health, lifestyle, makeup, fitness, unbiased news, books, self-help content or even alluring coffee-making videos – you have it all at your disposal.

All the profiles that you follow online, the ones that motivate you, educate you, entertain you, the ones that make you laugh and give you a sense of peace: favourite them. Turn your notifications to keep up to speed with all their new posts. This will not only help you, but the increased engagement will help them continue to create content and share their invaluable insight with all their followers.

People have the power to move you, encourage you and inspire you with words, images and videos that they are sharing online. All you need to do is open yourself up to it.

If you can't switch off social media apps entirely, then switch on the best ones and learn something from them.

Through consuming online content, your beliefs about how to apply self-love in your life can be distorted. One way to deal with this is to sit down and think about what makes you happy.

Maybe create a mood board, or brainstorm some ideas, or just reflect on what your happiest day this week was and think about what you did.

What does an ideal day of self-care look like to you, and you only?

MANIFEST A SAFE ONLINE SPACE

You might still struggle. You might still have the urge to search for that social media influencer with the hourglass figure and a boyfriend who models for Abercrombie and Fitch, or for the influencer who is always on holiday, or for Jess from school who married your high school sweetheart and is living the life you dreamed of. The issue is this: unless we create an online environment where people can comfortably share their negative experiences as well as their positive, we won't be completely free from social media comparison.

We're partly to blame for the social media problem.

We've created an online culture where people don't feel comfortable sharing their vulnerabilities. The fear of backlash, criticism or the possibility of being made the butt of a joke pushes people further away from being honest about their experiences, hence the constant filtered photos and videos on social media. The amount of hate from the keyboard warriors and online trolls that are everywhere makes being raw and vulnerable an anxiety-inducing experience.

Ask yourself this: if Jess from school posted a video of herself in tears over the problems in her marriage, would you not be taken aback? Would you not internally judge her? Would you not send her video to your WhatsApp group and make jabs such as 'attention-seeker' or 'why is she putting this online?'

And even if you didn't, even if you're a saint of non-judgement and wouldn't dream of talking badly about someone, you might still feel uncomfortable. You might feel second-hand embarrassment when you see that video. You might feel sorry for her. But she doesn't need pity, she needs to feel safe in sharing her vulnerabilities online, because online is where we all are.

Although we criticise the way people share the best parts of their life, we're also not entirely supportive when they are honest. I believe that we're making progress towards openness and vulnerability online, but there is still only a small amount of people who are completely honest and open. The rest of us still hide behind virtual filters.

When I first started my Instagram page, I had goosebumps every time I posted a poem. I was using a pseudonym, and I had blocked dozens of people from my community. The reason? Fear of judgement, of being made fun of, of being talked about. Eventually I overcame this fear. I unblocked everyone and started using my real name because I wanted to create a safe space for my readers to also be vocal about their weaknesses. I wanted my readers to feel protected in our community, and the only way I could do this is if I also felt protected online.

I started sharing my weaknesses and insecurities and being una-bashedly honest, and instead of being embarrassed, I found my strength in my honesty. It's simple: when you express your insecurities to people in a tone of voice that indicates you're embarrassed by them, you're giving others power to use your insecurities against you. But the moment you start voicing your insecurities as traits that are a part of you in a tone of voice, or language, that doesn't portray them as something to be embarrassed by, you're regaining your power.

> One way we can overcome the social media comparison problem is by working on our insecurities or accepting them so that we don't get triggered by other people's happiness. Another way is by creating the kind of online spaces that make it easy to have difficult conversations, where our insecurities are no longer our weakness.

IS THERE A SOLUTION?

While there is no categorical solution to the social media problem, there are some things you can do when you're on the path to self-love:

* *Limit your use of social media. You can either limit this to, e.g., 30–60 minutes a day or aim for one entire day each week without a phone. In the beginning this will be difficult, and you might need to use the settings in your phone to restrict your usage of social media apps. You can even try*

alternating between removing different apps to see if you feel better.

Reducing your use of social media will allow you to spend quality time with yourself without any distractions and become more comfortable in your presence.

✳ Use social media apps to connect with your family and friends or to access useful tools and resources. Social media is phenomenal for connecting people from all around the world, something we saw at length during the Covid-19 lockdowns. The power of social media to unite us, keep us sane and provide an escape from the loneliness we experienced during lockdown was astonishing.

✳ Remind yourself that social media is curated. No one always looks that perfect. No one's house is always pristine. No one has children who aren't little monsters at some point (take it from me, my little brother is a nightmare 80 per cent of the time, **but** he is also adorable). Social media is not real.

Also remember this when I'm posting way too many photos of this book when it comes out. I'll be living my best life, sure, but you don't know the blood, sweat and tears that have gone into making this book what it is.

✳ Unfollow profiles that make you feel bad about yourself. My motto has always been that if they're not adding to your life, then they don't need to be in your life, especially your 'social media friends'. Unfollowing them will do you better than harm, and – trust me – they won't even notice it.

✳ Work on your insecurities. Why does coming across someone else's photo make you feel bad about yourself? Do *they have something that you want? If yes, then figure out a plan for how to achieve it, or, if that's not possible, how to cope with not having that thing. If no, then what is it that is affecting you? If it's because you're unhappy in your life and seeing someone else's happiness is triggering for you, then do some self-reflective work so you're better at handling such cases.*

Ups and downs are a part of everyone's life, and if you're triggered by other people's success every time you have a failure of your own, it will damage your self-esteem highly. Make sure to remind yourself daily that you're on your own individual journey and the only person to compare yourself to is your former self.

Lastly, be kinder to yourself. The path to self-love is a long, beautiful journey that you're on. Remind yourself of how far you've come and be patient with yourself. Today might have been difficult, but tomorrow will be better. It will be better.

exercise

What does an ideal social media app when you're healing look like to you?

Draw a bubble with arrows pointing out and write/draw/doodle all the features that you'd like to see in a social media app that helps you on your self-love journey.

chapter 9

i'm loving myself and i'm healing

The path to self-love is life-changing. This path equips you with confidence to put yourself first. It gives you insight into the root of your insecurities. It encourages you to move on from your past trauma through both tough and easy self-love practices and it puts you in a favourable position where you can make the most of your experiences, enjoy fruitful relationships and live your best, happiest life. There's so much to this magnificent yet at times messy course which can change your life forever, if you let it.

exercise

At the start of this book, I asked you to think about something that you were struggling with in your healing which you would like to overcome by the end of the book. For example:

'I struggle with putting my foot down and saying no.'

'I can't move on from the person who broke my heart.'

'I don't know what I deserve.'

'A friend is hurting me, and I don't know how to tell her.'

'I'm grieving the death of a family member.'

'I realised I'm experiencing emotional abuse, and I don't know how to deal with it.'

'I recently lost my job, and it's caused me to have low self-esteem.'

I now want you to return to this struggle and think about the useful tools you've been equipped with in this book. Here is a recap of a few of them:

✳︎ *How to cultivate a relationship of self-love with yourself.*

✳︎ *How to harness the power of healthy relationships.*

✳︎ *How to use your support circle.*

✳︎ *How to set boundaries using communication and body language.*

✳︎ *When to let someone go, e.g., toxic friends.*

✳︎ *When to redeem the relationship, e.g., in cases of subtle emotional abuse.*

✳︎ *How to practise tough self-love.*

✳︎ *How to practise easy self-love.*

✳︎ *How to change harmful narratives.*

✳   *How to refrain from comparison.*

✳   *How to use social media as a communicative tool.*

✳   *How to accept change.*

There are many other tips and life hacks in this book, and I suggest that to truly make use of them, you try to complete all the journal prompts and exercises up to this point, if you haven't finished them all.

Now, using this book as your guide, create a solution for your struggle.

If more struggles come to mind – when you're walking on the path to self-love you will face many obstacles – return to the tools, journal prompts and exercises in this book to build a way out that works for you.

Self-love: my month summarised

I wrote my daily affirmations. Emailed them to myself and filed them away in a folder. I woke up earlier but let myself sleep in too. Made myself protein smoothies and calorie counted for two weeks straight before buying a pack of warm chocolate chip cookies and sharing them with my friends. I went on walks. Through long, leafy parks and bright, yellow streets. I wrapped myself up with a warm wool fleece and borrowed gloves, with a piping hot latte in one hand and my lover's fingers threaded through the other. I read more. Cute YA romance novels and steamy fantasy ones, but I still couldn't bring myself to read the heavy stuff. Picked up the self-help book on my desk a few times before flicking through the pages and grabbing my phone instead. I indulged in the latest Netflix series and watched lots of movies. I shopped a little, danced a lot and met new people after a long time, the nervousness bubbling in my stomach on the first two occasions, but settling down by the third. My mind wandered on many days. Sometimes I'd do a lot and feel tired. Sometimes, I'd do nothing at all and still feel the exhaustion hanging over my shoulders. I practised self-love in new ways because I no longer remembered the old. And after giving my mind and body a break, I decided to do something productive. I worked hard for the future and enjoyed the present, and each day was a blessing in disguise.

What Is Your Self-Love Manifesto?

Think about your individual self-love manifesto. There are things that this book has taught you, many things, but the one core facet of the path to self-love is that it looks different for everyone, even if you all take the same lessons from this book. Your experiences are unique. Individual to you. Your healing journey is as rare as your DNA and the self-love path that you take on that journey will be the one that you, *and only you*, need.

So, consider this path. Envision what you want from it. What do you see when you think of living your best, most content life? Is there anyone you picture in this life of yours? What about your career? Your health goals? Have you dealt with your trauma? Or are you still learning? Growing? Changing? Have you let go of the ones who never loved you and accepted new love, or are you peacefully alone? In your own presence. Enjoying the tranquillity of solitude.

Now, write a self-love manifesto that's designed for you, and you only.

In this manifesto, consider how self-love can help you realise all your goals for the ideal life you have in mind above. Consider how you can take care of yourself on a daily or a weekly basis, so you can be closer to achieving your happiest life.

If this means getting closure from an ex, include it. If it means reaching out to your mum after not speaking to her for two years, write it down. If it means going to the gym every day or learning how to practise yoga, note it down and don't forget it. If it means getting therapy, cutting people off, changing your career path or finally sticking up for yourself, put it all in your manifesto.

In this declaration of self-love, think about all the tough and easy self-love practices that can improve your life and add them in. Then, go ahead and incorporate this declaration into your day-to-day actions. Perhaps even write a 'Self-love: my month summarised' at the end of each month, like the one I've written on page 261. Follow this up with an additional one at the end of the year.

Keeping track of your habits will also allow you to see what's working for you and what isn't. You will notice who helps you grow and who makes you unhappy. You will see which questions still need to be answered and which have been dealt with. You will learn how life-changing the path to self-love truly is.

If you need some inspiration, re-read my 'Self-love: a month summarised' and use it as stimulus to write one of your own.

It's time for you to write your own self-love manifesto.

_____
_____
_____
_____
_____
_____
_____
_____
_____
_____
_____
_____
_____
_____
_____
_____
_____
_____
_____
_____
_____
_____
_____
_____
_____
_____

I LOVE MYSELF, BUT I DON'T DRINK MATCHA TEA LATTES

I love myself, but I don't drink matcha tea lattes or wake up at 6am for yoga. I wake up at a time that suits me and head to the gym, on most days. I love myself, but I don't go for an early morning run in the park or make healthy overnight oats, or meal prep for the entire week. I go on walks whenever I can. I read books. I listen to podcasts. I try to keep my protein up because I'm committed to improving how confident I am in my body, and controlling what I put inside my body makes me feel powerful, but I'm not strict with my diet.

I love myself, but I haven't gone on a soul-searching trip by myself, and perhaps I never will. But I've gone travelling with people who make me the happiest girl ever. I've experienced a ball of warmth where my heart is as I pelted my friends with squashed tomatoes at the Tomatina festival in a crowded street in Buñol, Spain, our laughter crackling through the air, meshing with the shrieks and shrills of thousands of others who joined in the festivities. I've felt the wind glide on my face, my arms wrapped around my husband's waist as he whizzed with his scooter through bright green and yellow rice fields in Bali, feeling more alive than I've ever felt before.

I love myself, but I'm not always nice to myself. I'm not even always nice to my loved ones because I can have bad days, but also because honesty can be bitter to the ears, and I prefer to be honest than kind. But I'm not shy to apologise. I'm not any less if I admit that I'm wrong.

I love myself but I don't wake up at the same time every day. I try to be consistent, but I'm not hard on myself if I don't live up to it.

I love myself and I've moved on from lots of past traumas, but I've never had therapy. I'd love to try, but I've read so many books and healing poetry over the years that a part of me has dealt with my past trauma. But if I experience any more, *because I'm certain there will be more*, then therapy is the first on my list.

I love myself, but I've never gone to a grief counselling session after being so affected by my mum's loss. I was young when I lost her and when I was old enough, mental health was too taboo a topic in my culture. And now, when it's easier to have mental health conversations, I've healed from that experience. I've made peace with it. But perhaps I'll give it a go one time, just to see if I still have anything left inside to say. I love myself but there are still lots of questions I need to answer. I've not *'found the answer'* to life's happiness, but I've developed ways to make myself happier and more content.

I love myself but I still compare my weaknesses to others. What can I say, I'm human after all. But I reflect. I understand that it isn't good, so I actively stop myself when I'm doing it. I love myself so I know that there are things that are good for me and things that are bad, and I need to fight the impulses that block me from disengaging from the bad and focusing on the good.

I hope you can see where I'm going with this.

My self-love journey is different to yours, and yours will be different to the next person's. In this journey, I've made a lot of progress, but I have a long way to go still, because healing is lifelong. You will move on from certain painful experiences and then have more, and that will set off new healing journeys.

Getting hurt, losing people, having uncomfortable experiences, facing your daily challenges and fighting your fears are all a part of the life that you will continue to live. These aspects of your day-to-day life don't just disappear. They are there, at every bend, every corner.

This path to self-love that you walk on isn't a 'solution' to your problems – instead it gives you the courage to face them. To deal with them. To learn to move forward with them. To become a better version of yourself. Because there will be more healing to go through in your future. And there will be hurt. And loss. And low self-esteem. These are the ups and downs of this existence that we're all fortunate enough to have. Self-love will encourage you to embrace every shade of life, with all its imperfections, and keep going. Keep going.

I love myself, but I'm still imperfect, flawed, messy and rough around the edges, and you might be too. Which is okay. Which is fine.

I'm an example of the fact that when you sit down to consider what self-love looks like in your life going forward, it might be nothing like what you thought it would be. But it will still be special. It will still be important to your individual path. It will still change your life for the better.

Why don't you give this a go too? Start with *'I love myself . . .'* and see what you come up with on the pages in front of you.

exercise

Where do you see yourself in:

    1 year
    5 years
    10 years

You can do this exercise in any way you want.

You can share this question with your friends on your next evening out and you can all express your goals to each other, basking in the tenderness of each other's encouragement as you share your vulnerable, delicate dreams.

Or write it down in a journal. Or email it to yourself, which is what I do, so you have it on file to look back at when you cross those milestones in your life.

Or film a video to your future self, telling them what you think life looks like for them at that time.

Or do your most creative painting/drawing/doodle ever, with all the things that you see for yourself in those periods of your life.

Then, go out and manifest this. Work hard. But remember to smile and be happy. This life is beautiful, it is a gift, so make the most of it while you can.

I'm Loving Myself and I'm Healing

The path to self-love has transformed my healing journey.

It's taken me years to reach this point where I know what works and what doesn't, and I'm confident that I can practise self-love. I've navigated my self-love journey through all the highs and lows of my healing. I've rewritten several of the negative narratives that I developed in my mind because of all the trauma that I faced. I can adequately balance my relationships with my self-love practice, especially my most valuable relationship – the one with my dad. I've removed people who aren't good for me and set boundaries with those that I want to keep in my life. I cherish my bond with my husband, Ivnit, and I make the most of our adventures together. I try – *on most days* – not to let filtered social media get to me, and I actively stop myself if I find that I'm comparing my lows to someone's highs.

I'm so grateful for this life, and I'm glad that I made the changes that I did. I'm doing better. I'm so much happier than I was before. A sense of peace and tranquillity has enveloped my life in a way that ten-year-old me would have never dreamed of. She was busy counting the stars on a ceiling, hoping to make a wish on one of them. If only she could see me now.

But life isn't all black and white, and you won't always be in a state of happiness or a state of gloom. The truth of existence is that some days are still harder than others. I'm human, after all. Sometimes I still find myself pondering the *could haves*, the *would haves*, the *should haves*. Sometimes I still worry about the home I've left behind, and the people within it. Sometimes the past still crawls in like a bad cold and stays for a while, shaking up everything on the inside before leaving. But what's changed from before is that I can manage the bad days better now.

After learning that self-love is personal to me, and accepting it in every bend of my experiences, I know how to take care of myself – even on the bad days. So, when the bad days come, I let them pass. I let them breathe. I let them stay. I even let them take me under. Because I know that I will come out the other side. I know that I will make it.

> *Self-love is magnificent. It changes your life forever. It gives you confidence. It inspires you. It moves you to do things for yourself. It allows you to accept all the good in your life and reject the bad. Self-love shapes your healing journey so that you can truly make progress. So that you can truly heal.*

If you've started healing or have been healing from one or more hurtful experiences for a while – firstly, I'm truly sorry for what you've gone through, but I'm confident that this book has given you the push that you need to kick-start your individual path to self-love, if you haven't already. But take it with a pinch of salt. Don't dive into the ocean of self-love before you've at least learned to float. And don't be mistaken. Some days will be harder than others, even when you think that you have it all figured out. And that is normal.

But this book will encourage you to face those days confidently. As long as you make sense of your personal self-love experience, as long as you figure out what works for you and what doesn't, as long as you practise self-love in a way that sustains you, in a way that respects the highs and lows of your life and your healing. I'm certain that – with time – the bad days won't affect you as much as they used to. In fact, I'm confident that you will do great.

When the bad days arrive, you might let them pass. You might let them breathe. You might let them stay with you for a while. You might even let them take you under, because you know that after the bad days, the good days will follow. You know that you will come out the other side. You know that you will make it.

All the best on your path to self-love.

Love, Ruby x

You will be okay. Close your eyes. Breathe. You will be fine. This day is hard, and tomorrow might be harder, but it will get easier soon. It must. So, just keep going. Keep hoping. Keep waking up each morning with the small glimmer of a smile that used to take up your entire face. Keep spending each night tucking away your fears into the pleats of a heart that has felt too much and know — <u>just know</u> — that one day you won't have to hide anymore. One day, the sun will cast a yellow glow so bright that it will light up everything that has dimmed inside you. One day, you will bite your lip as you see your reflection in the mirror and feel a kindle of happiness, your cheeks slowly bundling up into a familiar grin that you haven't seen for a while. One day, you won't have to force yourself to get out of bed — <u>it will feel easier to</u>. So, just know that it will be okay. You will be okay. Because there have been many moments like this one, moments where you felt helpless, and there have been many storms in the past like this one, storms that you never thought you could come through — but you survived. You survived.

Acknowledgements

Writing this book has been the hardest and most fulfilling thing I've ever done, and it wouldn't have been possible without the people who have been beside me every step of the way.

To my family: we've gone through so much together. We've had highs and lows, we've laughed, cried and felt the trembles of existence and still come through, with our strong love for each other keeping us going. Without those moments I shared with you I wouldn't be where I am today, without the pieces of you that you handed to me I would fail to exist. So, thank you for everything.

Thank you to my dad, who always tries his best. Thank you for the daily fresh juices, for the lifelong drop-offs and pick-ups, for taking care of me whenever I was ill, for cooking my favourite food, for being both the mum and the dad in my life, for telling me all the stories that I will pass to my children one day. Thank you for not giving up. I know that life hasn't been easy for you, but every time you face one more day with a smile on your face, I'm given the courage to keep going too.

Thank you to both my brothers. Veer: who will forever be my first child and my baby. And to Ricky: you are my idol, my rock, and my best friend in the entire world. Without you, I wouldn't have survived any of this. Thank you for never giving up on me. Thank you for always pushing me to follow my dreams. You're the best brother anyone could ask for.

Thank you to my husband, Ivnit. There aren't enough words to describe what I feel for you. All I can say is that you are every dream about love I've had come true. You have changed the trajectory of my life and brought me so much happiness. You being here beside me, every step along the way, makes this journey called life so much more beautiful. You bring light to my days and the stars to my nights, and constant peace to my heart. Your unwavering love, support and faith in me has pushed me to reach for the stars. Thank you for giving me the family I always dreamt of. Thank you for being you.

I'd also like to thank all the people who made this book happen.

Vex King: your compassion for creatives like me is admirable. If you hadn't believed in me, none of this would have come true. Thank you for being the catalyst in this journey.

To my agent Jane: you are kind, wise, passionate and so inspiring. I appreciate everything that you've done for me and this book.

Thank you to the entire team at Penguin Random House. I've dreamt of being published by you for as long as I can remember. This moment is a ten-year-old girl's dream come true – *it's so, so special to me*. Thank you for giving me the honour of writing a book with you. I'd also like to thank you for all the work you've put into this book. I won't be able to name everyone individually, but I'd like to thank a few people in particular: Evangeline Stanford, Sam Jackson, Donna Loffredo, Katherine Leak, Jessica Anderson, Ellie Crisp and Shikha Jajoo, and anyone else that I have failed to mention but whose contribution to this book is invaluable.

I appreciate the constant support, the brilliant feedback, the earnest answers to all my emails, and for always having a smile on your faces and for being super encouraging and accommodating. You're all absolute stars.

Finally, thank you to my lovebugs: my readers. Your constant love and support motivate me to continue writing and sharing my art with the world. You have saved me many times over the years, and I hope that this book saved you in some way too. I love you all so much.